# LITTLE KNOWN FACTS
## ABOUT
## WELL KNOWN PEOPLE

# LITTLE KNOWN FACTS ABOUT WELL KNOWN PEOPLE

### By Dale Carnegie
*Author of "The Unknown Lincoln," etc.*

**BLUE RIBBON BOOKS**
*New York*

Copyright 1934 by
GREENBERG, PUBLISHER, Inc.

PRINTED IN THE UNITED STATES OF AMERICA

## CONTENTS

The Wizard Einstein Was Once the School Dunce . 1

The Man Who Was Robbed of a Billion Dollars . . 7

The Poet Who Married a Child and Got Ten Dollars for Ten Years' Work . . . . . . 13

Cleopatra Won the Love of Two of the Greatest Leaders Who Ever Lived . . . . . . 17

The Glamorous Garbo Used to Work in a Barber Shop . . . . . . . . . . 25

The Pillows of the Crown Prince Were Stained with Blood . . . . . . . . . 31

They Tried to Shoot Marconi for Inventing Radio . 35

She Ruled an Empire, Married an Imbecile, and Had a Score of Lovers . . . . . . . . 41

The Punctual Napoleon Kept Her Waiting Two Hours at the Altar . . . . . . . 45

He Changed the World's History But Got No Thrill out of It . . . . . . . . . 51

He Made a Fortune out of a Mouse and Three Pigs . 55

He Ruled One Sixth of the World—and Was Shot in a Dirty Cellar . . . . . . . . 61

The World's Best Known Man Carries False Teeth in His Loin Cloth . . . . . . . 65

The Navy Couldn't Use Him But He Is Now Our Most Famous Admiral . . . . . . 71

## CONTENTS

| | |
|---|---|
| HE WAS ASHAMED OF HAVING WRITTEN ONE OF THE MOST FAMOUS BOOKS IN THE WORLD | 75 |
| HE USES BAD ENGLISH BUT HE GETS FIVE DOLLARS A SECOND FOR TALKING | 77 |
| THE BEST KNOWN RADIO PREACHER IN THE WORLD HAS A "WICKED" BIBLE | 83 |
| HE WROTE 1200 VOLUMES AND BOASTED THAT HE HAD 500 CHILDREN | 87 |
| A CYCLONE IN PETTICOATS WHO STARTLED AMERICA | 93 |
| THE RICHEST MAN IN THE WORLD EATS SOUP WITH HIS FINGERS | 99 |
| ONCE HE SLEPT IN A PACKING BOX—TODAY HE IS WORSHIPPED AS A GOD | 105 |
| HE MADE THOUSANDS OF MILLIONAIRES AND DIED WITH HOLES IN HIS SHOES | 109 |
| HE GOT A QUARTER OF A MILLION TELEGRAMS IN LESS THAN AN HOUR | 115 |
| COLUMBUS WAS THE THIRD MAN TO DISCOVER AMERICA | 119 |
| SHE SANG IN OLD LACE CURTAINS AND WROTE THE MOST POPULAR SONG OF THE 20TH CENTURY | 125 |
| HE LOVES TO BE CALLED THE BIGGEST LIAR IN THE WORLD | 129 |
| SHE DROVE A BATTERED OLD CAR INTO LOS ANGELES AND MADE A MILLION IN 18 MONTHS | 135 |
| THE MOST WIDELY READ LIVING AUTHOR WENT HUNGRY FOR YEARS | 141 |
| THE BIGGEST FAKER IN AMERICA WAS FOOLED AGAIN AND AGAIN | 145 |
| A MAN WHO ATE SHOESTRINGS—AND LIKED THEM | 151 |
| HE DREAMED OF PUNCHING COWS WHILE YANKING TEETH | 155 |

## CONTENTS

Mrs. Lincoln Flung Hot Coffee in Abraham's Face . . 161

He Hates Crowds But He Has an Audience of 20,000,000 People a Day . . . . . . . 165

Christ Was not Born on Christmas Day . . . . 171

The Grand Duchess Who Married so she Could Wear Silk Stockings . . . . . . . . . . 175

The Man Who Was Swept out to Sea on an Ice-floe 179

A Great Author Who Was Bored by Her Own Masterpiece . . . . . . . . . . . . 185

Woolworth's Boss Paid Him No Salary Because He Was so Dumb . . . . . . . . . . 189

A Gang of Counterfeiters Tried to Steal Lincoln's Body . . . . . . . . . . . . . 193

If H. G. Wells Hadn't Broken His Leg He Might Still Be Clerking in a Drygoods Store . . . . . 199

Mozart's Funeral Cost $3.10—and No One Followed His Coffin to the Grave . . . . . . . . 205

He Revolutionized Music But He Still Takes Three Lessons a Week . . . . . . . . . . 209

They Spent Their Lives Keeping the Big Bad Wolf Away . . . . . . . . . . . . . 213

He Had Twenty-seven Wives and Made Twenty-six of Them Knit Their Own Garters . . . . . 219

He Slept with Each Leg of His Bed in Salt to Keep Evil Spirits Away . . . . . . . . . 225

She Wrote Mystery Stories—so the Ghosts Decided to Move Right in . . . . . . . . . . 229

Thomas Edison Wasn't the Only Smart Man with a Bad Memory . . . . . . . . . . . 235

They Went to Jail—and It Added to Their Greatness 243

## LIST OF ILLUSTRATIONS

| | |
|---|---|
| Albert Einstein | 2 |
| General Sutter | 6 |
| Edgar Allan Poe | 12 |
| Cleopatra | 18 |
| Greta Garbo | 24 |
| Crown Prince Rudolf | 30 |
| Marconi | 36 |
| Catherine the Great of Russia | 40 |
| Josephine | 46 |
| Orville Wright | 50 |
| Walt Disney | 56 |
| Nicholas II | 60 |
| Mahatma Gandhi | 66 |
| Admiral Richard Byrd | 70 |
| Rev. Charles L. Dodgson | 74 |
| William Penn Adair Rogers | 78 |
| Dr. S. Parkes Cadman | 82 |
| Alexander Dumas | 88 |
| Carry Nation | 94 |
| Nizam of Hyderabad | 100 |
| Lenin | 104 |
| John Law | 110 |
| Lowell Thomas | 114 |

## LIST OF ILLUSTRATIONS

| | |
|---|---:|
| Christopher Columbus | 120 |
| Carrie Jacobs Bond | 124 |
| Robert L. Ripley | 130 |
| Aimee Semple McPherson Hutton | 136 |
| Upton Sinclair | 140 |
| P. T. Barnum | 146 |
| Vilhjalmur Stefansson | 150 |
| Zane Grey | 156 |
| Mrs. Abraham Lincoln | 160 |
| O. O. McIntyre | 166 |
| Merry Old Santa Claus | 172 |
| Grand Duchess Marie | 176 |
| Sir Wilfred Grenfell | 180 |
| Louisa May Alcott | 184 |
| F. W. Woolworth | 188 |
| Abe Lincoln's Body | 194 |
| H. G. Wells | 200 |
| Mozart | 204 |
| George Gershwin | 208 |
| Mark Twain | 214 |
| Brigham Young | 218 |
| Cornelius Vanderbilt | 224 |
| Mary Roberts Rinehart | 230 |
| Thomas A. Edison | 234 |
| O. Henry | 242 |

# THE WIZARD EINSTEIN WAS ONCE THE SCHOOL DUNCE

I WAS walking down the streets of a little town in Southern Germany a few years ago when a friend who was with me suddenly stopped and pointed to a window over a grocery store and said: "See that little apartment up there? That is where Einstein was born."

Later that day, I met Einstein's uncle and talked to him. But he didn't impress me as being a man of any unusual ability. But that isn't strange, for when Albert Einstein himself was a child, no one thought he would amount to much either. He is now regarded as the outstanding intellectual giant of this generation, one of the most profound thinkers of all time; yet fifty years ago, he was a slow, shy, backward child. He found it extremely difficult to learn even to talk. He was so dull that his own teachers called him a bore, and even his parents feared that he was subnormal.

Einstein was astonished to wake up a few years ago and find himself one of the most famous men on all the earth. It seemed absolutely incredible that a professor of mathematics had become front page news on five continents. He, a scientist, has become as famous as Jack Dempsey. He admits he can't understand it. No one can understand it. Such a thing has never happened before in all the annals of mankind.

This man Einstein is almost as strange as his Theory of Relativity. He has nothing but contempt for the things

*Lithograph by Rothenstein*
**ALBERT EINSTEIN**
His teachers despaired; he even learned to talk with difficulty

## ABOUT WELL KNOWN PEOPLE

most people set their hearts on—for fame and riches and luxury. For example, the captain of a transatlantic ship once offered Einstein the most expensive suite of rooms on the vessel; but Einstein declined and said he would rather travel in the steerage than accept any special favors.

When Einstein reached his fiftieth birthday, Germany overwhelmed him with honors, erected a bust of him at Potsdam, and offered him a home and a sail boat as a token of the nation's love and undying admiration.

But now, a few years later, his property has been taken away from him and he is afraid to return to his native land. For weeks he lived in Belgium behind barred doors and a policeman slept at his bedside every night.

When he arrived in New York to become Professor of Mathematics in the Institute for Advanced Study at Princeton, he was anxious to avoid reporters and interviews and excitement; so his friends took him off the ship secretly before it docked and hurried him away by automobile.

Einstein says that there are only twelve people living who understand his Theory of Relativity, although more than nine hundred books have been written attempting to explain it.

He himself explains Relativity by this very simple illustration: when you sit with a nice girl for an hour, you think it is only a minute; but when you sit on a hot stove for a minute, you think it is an hour.

Well, well so that's relativity. It sounds all right to me; but if you doubt it and would like to try it out, I'll be glad to sit with the girl if you'll sit on the stove.

And speaking of girls, Einstein has been married twice. He has two boys by his first marriage, both brilliant chaps with the earmarks of genius.

Mrs. Einstein admits that even she doesn't understand the Theory of Relativity; but she understands something that is far more important for a wife; she understands her husband.

She used to invite her friends in for tea occasionally and then she would ask the Professor to come downstairs and join them. "No!" he would exclaim violently. "No! *I won't! I won't!* I'm going away from here. I can't work here. I simply won't stand these interruptions any longer."

Frau Einstein would keep perfectly quiet until he had blown off steam for awhile; and then, presently, by using a little diplomacy, she would have him downstairs drinking tea and getting some much-needed relaxation.

Frau Einstein says that her husband likes order in his thinking, but he doesn't like it in his living. He does whatever he wants to, whenever he wants to. And he has only two rules of conduct. The first one is: Don't have any rules whatever. And the second one is: Be independent of the opinions of others.

He leads a very simple sort of an existence, goes around in old clothes that need pressing, seldom wears a hat, and whistles and sings in the bathroom. He shaves while sitting in the bath tub and he doesn't use shaving soap. He shaves with the same soap that he uses for his bath. This man who is trying to solve the vexing riddles of the universe says that using two kinds of soap makes life entirely too complicated. Einstein impresses me as being a very happy man. His philosophy of happiness means far more to me than does his Theory of Relativity. I think it a splendid philosophy. He says he is happy because he doesn't want anything from anybody. He doesn't want money or titles or praise. He makes his own happiness out of such

# ABOUT WELL KNOWN PEOPLE

simple things as his work and playing the violin and sailing his boat.

Einstein's violin brings him more joy than anything else in life. He says he often thinks in music and lives his day dreams in music.

Once, while riding a street car in Berlin, he told the conductor that he hadn't given him the right change. The conductor counted the change again and found it to be correct, so he handed it back to Einstein saying: "The trouble with you is, you don't know figures."

*Courtesy of Harper Brothers*

GENERAL SUTTER

He died in rags, his only possession a deed to the greatest fortune on earth

# THE MAN WHO WAS ROBBED OF
## A BILLION DOLLARS

OUT in California, on January 24, 1848, John W. Marshall, a carpenter, was building a grist mill on the South fork of the American River; and on this particular day, he stooped and picked up a small yellow stone that had been washed down from the wooded hills above the present city of Sacramento. Was it gold? He couldn't tell. So he gave it to a workman's wife who was boiling some home-made soap. She tossed the stone into the kettle of boiling fat and lye.

After being cooked all day, the nugget gleamed like a tiger's eye; and the next morning at daybreak, John W. Marshall leaped on his horse and hurried pell-mell forty miles down the canyon to the ranch house of his employer, John A. Sutter.

Marshall rushed into the house, locked the door and pulled the yellow nugget from his pocket. Sutter stared at it, wide-eyed with excitement.

It was gold and he knew it. A pure nugget of glistening gold. His wildest dreams had been transcended. He would soon be lord of all creation, the richest man in the world.

Sutter attempted to keep the discovery a secret; but he might as well have tried to prevent the very stars from shining in their orbits. He had unleashed a force that was destined to shake the continent. Within a day, all the men on Sutter's ranch left their appointed tasks and, in a mad frenzy of greed, they were scratching and digging and panning for gold.

In a week, the whole countryside was in a turmoil. Ranches were deserted. Everything was in chaos. Cows were left bellowing to be milked. Calves bawled in vain for their mothers, while wolves slaughtered the bleating sheep.

Excited men, with pick and shovels, were soon making from a thousand to five thousand dollars between sunrise and sunset. One cut of the spade and a couple of shakes of the sieve and presto! nuggets worth thousands of dollars lay at your feet—a fortune made in a minute.

Telegraph wires flashed the sensational news across the continent and convulsed the nation with excitement. Workmen left their shops, soldiers deserted from the army by wholesale, farmers abandoned their lands, merchants locked their stores. The gold diggers were on the move. The locust swarm of humanity took wings and headed for the golden land beyond the sunset.

In the Spring of 1849, a mighty cavalcade trekked out of Independence, Kansas, the last outpost of civilization. Youth was in the saddle, youth thrilling to the quest of a new adventure. From the Missouri River to the snow-packed summits of the Sierra Nevadas, there flowed a long, unbroken line of wagon trains, drawn by horses and slow-moving oxen. The prairie was riotously green with spring and rollicking songs rolled from wagon train to wagon train.

Countless thousands of others were coming by sea. Packed into whaling ships and cargo boats, they rounded Cape Horn under whining sails and creaking masts.

Smashed and pounded by hurricanes off the Straits of Magellan, racked by raging fevers, smitten with scurvy, their ranks decimated by cholera, the gold diggers sailed on, as irresistible as the sweep of the mighty Pacific.

In the hectic year 1849, more than seven hundred vessels dropped anchor in San Francisco Bay, and the sailors immediately deserted their ships and rushed to the hills.

It was a mob, a rabble, that recognized no law but the law of the knife and the club, and obeyed no orders unless they were backed up by guns.

Naturally, the mob converged from all sides on Sutter's ranch. They trampled his grain under foot and they stole his wheat to make bread. They demolished his barns to build shanties and they slaughtered his cattle to get steaks.

What was even more astonishing, these treasure hunters even had the audacity to build towns on the private property of John A. Sutter; and the old rancher looked on in helpless rage while strange men bought and sold and resold his land as if he had never existed.

In 1850, Californa was ushered into the Union, and the majestic order of law now ruled over the turbulent hills.

Then Sutter started the biggest law suit in history. He declared that San Francisco and Sacramento were both built on his private property and he prosecuted every "squatter" living in those towns and ordered them to get off his land at once. He sued the State of California for twenty-five million dollars as compensation for the private roads and bridges and canals that he had built and the State had appropriated for public use.

He demanded that the United States Government pay him fifty million dollars for the damages he had suffered;

and he also demanded that he be paid a royalty for every dollar's worth of gold dust that had been carried away from his property.

For four years he fought the case through court after court, and in 1855, he won. The highest court in the State of California declared that the cities of San Francisco and Sacramento, and scores of other towns and villages, were built on his private property.

The news of this sensational decision rocked the inhabitants of San Francisco and Sacramento like an earthquake. So the law was going to put them out of their homes, was it? Well, they would show the law a thing or two! A milling mob, driven mad by desperation, grabbed guns and axes and torches and marched through the streets, yelling and sacking and looting and burning.

They set fire to the law courts, and burned up the records; then they got a rope and tried to lynch the judge who had rendered the decision. Leaping on their horses, they dashed away to Sutter's ranch, put sticks of dynamite under his houses and barns and blew his buildings high into the sky. They burned his furniture. They cut down his fruit trees. They shot his cattle. They turned his fertile ranch into a place of smoking desolation.

They murdered one of Sutter's sons. They drove another one to commit suicide; and the third son was drowned while attempting to get to Europe. John A. Sutter himself, staggering under these cruel blows, lost his reason.

For twenty years after that, he haunted the Capitol at Washington, trying to persuade Congress to recognize his rights. Dressed in rags, the poor, old, demented man went from one Senator to another, pleading for justice; and the children in the street laughed and jeered at him as he passed.

In the Spring of 1880, he died alone in a furnished room in Washington. Died, neglected and despised by those who had filched millions from his land. He didn't have a dollar when he passed away, but he did have a legal deed to the greatest fortune on earth.

Five years later, John W. Marshall passed on—Marshall, the carpenter, whose discovery had started the most gigantic gold rush in the history of the Western World. He died alone in his squalid cabin. Other men had made a thousand million dollars out of his discovery, but he didn't leave enough money to pay for a cheap coffin.

**EDGAR ALLAN POE**
At twenty-six, he was twice as old as his wife

# THE POET WHO MARRIED A CHILD AND GOT TEN DOLLARS FOR TEN YEARS' WORK

EDGAR ALLAN POE was one of the most striking and romantic geniuses that ever wrote a sonnet or concocted a mystery. He was destined to stride like a melancholy giant across the pages of American literature. Yet he was removed from the University of Virginia because of his wild passion for gambling and drinking; and later on, he was court-martialed and kicked out of West Point because he ignored all rules and sat in his quarters writing poetry when he ought to have been out on the parade ground drilling with a gun.

Poe was left an orphan early in life, and adopted by a rich tobacco merchant. Finally, even this merchant turned against his adopted son, beat him with a cane, drove him out of the house, disinherited him, and refused to leave him a dollar in his will.

The story of Poe's marriage is one of the most beautiful tales in literature. He married his first cousin, Virginia Clem. He had no money at the time. He *never had had* any money and he *never would have* any money. He drank raw alcohol. His only sister had gone crazy, and some people accused him of being half mad. And he was twice as old as his young wife. He was twenty-six and she was thirteen. According to all the old copy-book adages, his marriage should have ended in swift and sure disaster.

But it didn't: It was a romantic success. Poe all but worshipped this child-wife of his, and his undying love for her inspired some of the most exquisite poetry that ever enriched the English language.

Edgar Allan Poe spun stories and created verses that were destined to be placed among the literary glories and treasures of the earth; and yet he couldn't sell these immortal masterpieces for enough to buy bread. For example, he gave the world a poem that has become immortal:

> And the raven, never flitting, still is sitting,
> > still is sitting
> On the pallid bust of Pallas, just above my
> > chamber door.
> And his eyes have all the seeming of a demon
> > that is dreaming,
> And the lamplight o'er him streaming throws
> > his shadow on the floor.

Poe wrote and rewrote and revised *The Raven,* and worked on it intermittently for ten years; and yet he had to sell it for only ten dollars—a dollar for each year's work.

John Barrymore, out in Hollywood, gets more than that for one minute of his services. Apparently, there is more money in pictures than in poetry.

Poe, as I said, got ten dollars for writing *The Raven;* and the original manuscript recently sold for tens of thousands of dollars. Why is it that we let our geniuses go hungry while they are living, and then pay fantastic prices for their handwriting when they are dead?

Up at the Grand Concourse, in New York, is the cottage where Poe and Virginia lived. When Poe rented the place eighty-eight years ago, it was just an old shack about to fall to pieces. Now it is surrounded by apartment houses; but then it was in the country, nestling among the apple trees; and when Spring crept up from the South, the air was redolent with the perfume of lilacs and cherry blossoms, and the air hummed with the buzzing of bees. It was a beautiful, dream-like spot.

Poe rented the place for three dollars a month; but he couldn't pay even that. Most of the time he didn't pay any rent at all. His wife was ill with consumption; and he couldn't even buy food for her. Sometimes they went for days and days without anything to eat at all. When the dandelions began to bloom in the yard, they picked them and boiled them and ate dandelions, day after day.

When the neighbors discovered that Poe and his wife were on the verge of actual starvation, they brought them baskets of food. Pitiful? Yes, but he had the gift of song, and she had the gift of loving—and so they were happy, in spite of their poverty.

Virginia died there, eighty-seven years ago; and for months before she died, she lay on a straw mattress without enough clothing to keep her warm. When she became too cold, her mother rubbed her hands and Poe rubbed her feet. Poe covered her shivering body with his old military cloak that he had worn at West Point, and at night, he coaxed the cat to sleep at her feet.

When she died, Poe didn't have enough money to bury her; and if it hadn't been for the kindness of a neighbor, she would have been sent to Potter's field.

Years ago, the State of New York purchased this cottage, and made it a shrine. To me, it is a dream-cottage, filled with haunting and melancholy memories, and I can hardly tear myself away from it.

Virginia died in January. Months passed, Spring came, the moon rose over the apple trees and the stars twinkled on the western horizon, but Poe sat and dreamed and longed for Virginia; and out of that longing, he wrote the most beautiful love tribute that any man ever paid to his wife:

> *For the moon never beams without bringing me*
>   *dreams of the beautiful Annabel Lee,*
> *And the stars never rise but I feel the bright*
>   *eyes, of the beautiful Annabel Lee.*
> *And so, all the night-tide, I lie down by the side*
>   *of my darling, my darling, my life and my*
>   *bride,*
> *In her sepulchre there by the sea,*
>   *In her tomb by the sounding sea.*

## CLEOPATRA WON THE LOVE OF TWO OF THE GREATEST LEADERS WHO EVER LIVED

THIS is a bit of the story of the most seductive sweetheart that ever raised a man's blood pressure. Her name was Cleopatra, the queen goddess of Egypt—Cleopatra, the enchantress of the Nile.

She has been dead for two thousand years, but her fame still glows brightly across the dead centuries. She committed suicide when she was thirty-nine; yet in her short riot of life, she won and held the ardent love of two of the most famous men who ever walked the earth—Mark Antony and Julius Caesar, the latter of whom you honor every time you speak of the month of July, which was named in his memory.

Caesar had conquered practically all the earth; but little Cleopatra conquered him, and the story of how she did it is one of the dramatic incidents of antiquity.

When Caesar drifted down to Alexandria, forty-eight years before the birth of Christ, Cleopatra was in a bad way. Her throne had been taken away from her, she had no money and she was in grave danger of having her head cut off. She had married her brother, they had had a family quarrel, he made war on her, and she had fled from Egypt to save her life.

Caesar commanded her to appear before him. But how

*Courtesy of Liberty Magazine*

### CLEOPATRA
She committed suicide at 39; yet she had won the love of two
of the most famous men who ever lived

could she? That was a problem, for Alexandria was infested with her brother's spies, and to be caught meant instant death. So one dark night, she slipped into the city in a small fishing boat, had her servant tie her up in a roll of carpet being shipped to the palace, and unroll it before the eyes of the mighty Caesar.

When Cleopatra leaped out of that carpet and started laughing and dancing around the room, the very sight of her exquisite body quickened the riotous blood of the astonished Caesar.

Boasting that he himself was descended from Venus, the goddess of Love, Caesar prided himself on being a judge of feminine pulchritude; but this was something new, something breath-taking.

"My! My!" Caesar might have said to himself, "*Oo, la, la,* how long has this been going on? Why haven't we girls like that in Rome?

Caesar was fifty-four and bald-headed, and Cleopatra was exuberant with the vitality of a youth of twenty-one; and as Caesar looked upon her, he was lifted, as if by a tidal wave, to the foamy crests of love and ecstasy. By the ardor of her passion and the brilliance of her mentality, she made Caesar her willing slave for life.

So this brother of hers was trying to kill her, was he? Well, Caesar swore that he would teach that young upstart a lesson; so, with his Roman legions, he marched out and annihilated the Egyptian army and chased her brother into the Nile where he was drowned.

From that time on, Cleopatra was the undisputed Queen of Egypt, holding dominion over all the lands of the Pharaohs.

Months went by, and Cleopatra presented Caesar with

a son—the only son he ever had. With one wife back in Rome, of course Caesar couldn't marry Cleopatra—you know how tongues will wag. So to hush up the scandal and legitimatize her son, Cleopatra used a brilliant piece of strategy. She ordered the priests to announce that Julius Caesar wasn't a man at all. No. No. He was a God. He was the reincarnation of Ammon, the Sun God, and he had come back to earth in Caesar's body to procreate a child for the Queen.

Sounds like a wild tale to me; but people believed it two thousand years ago in Egypt. I am afraid that Cleopatra would have a hard time getting by with that story now.

Shortly after that, Caesar was assassinated; and roaring old Mark Antony, always drunk, always in debt, became the mightiest Roman of them all. Intoxicated with the wine of victory, Mark Antony led his armies into the East, bent on loot and plunder and a life of dissipation.

Egypt was the richest country in the East; so some of Antony's followers said to him when he was sober: "Look here, let's go down to Alexandria, cut off Cleopatra's head and feast on the flesh pots of Egypt."

Cleopatra trembled. How could she stop Antony? With ships and swords? Never. With love and caresses? Yes, may be. So with a flair for the dramatic, with a genius for showmanship, she set out to meet Antony in a gilded ship with purple sails. Surrounding herself with all the pomp and pageantry of the Arabian Nights, she had little boys, painted as Cupids, fanning her with peacock feathers, while voluptuous maidens, swathed in silk, danced to the wild strains of desert music. The fragrance of burning incense intoxicated the senses; and, in the midst of all this oriental glamour, Cleopatra lay on a silken couch, enchanting, irresistible, posing as Venus, the Goddess of Love.

Well, now, there you are. What would you have done if you had been Mark Antony? Well, that is precisely what I would have done too. Why, if Mark Antony had been down in bed with rheumatism and dyspepsia and dandruff, he couldn't have resisted a girl like that. He didn't even try.

A rough, crude, vulgar soldier was this man Antony, giving wild parties to wild women and mountebanks, and scandalizing even Rome. And now, Cleopatra, a woman to the manor born, a creature of culture and refinement, a woman who could quote poetry, had become his mistress. His passion for her brought into his boisterous life the first touch of beauty and sublimity he had ever known, and it inspired in him a devotion and fidelity that commands our admiration across more than twenty centuries.

Cleopatra knew how to handle men. She didn't nag about his manners. She did everything he wanted to do. She shot dice with him, hunted and fished with him; and sometimes, she even disguised herself as a slave and strolled through the streets at night with him, jerking chairs from under people and playing wild pranks. Once, when they were out fishing, and Antony complained because he didn't get any "bites," Cleopatra had one of her servants swim under the ship and put a salt herring on Antony's hook.

Cleopatra catered to Mark's stomach and always kept a retinue of chefs on constant duty, day and night, preparing hot dishes, so that a sumptuous banquet could be served the instant Antony desired it.

Antony became so infatuated with her that he lost all semblance of sense. He gave her the whole sea coast of Phoenicia as a present. Then he made her a gift of the province of Jericho, the island of Cyprus, the island of Creto. Finally, as a grand climax to all his lavishness, he handed over to her the whole province of Asia.

The news of these gifts set Rome seething with hate and boiling with fury. What? Was all this territory, bought with a hundred battles and paid for in Roman blood, to be tossed away like a bauble to satisfy the whims of an Egyptian mistress? The answer was WAR. Cleopatra's hour had struck. She had overplayed her hand. The day of awful reckoning had come, and Rome rose in its mighty wrath, destroyed the ships of Antony and Cleopatra and routed their armies.

This was the end, and they knew it. Antony realized that he would be captured and beheaded, so he stabbed himself and died writhing in agony in the arms of Cleopatra, clinging to her in death as he had clung to her in life.

She vowed over and over again that she would never be taken captive and led through the streets of Rome in chains for the populace to hoot and jeer at. So she committed suicide by poisoning. How she did it, no one will ever know. Even the people who found her, twenty minutes after she died, couldn't solve the mystery. Some thought she had bitten herself and then poured the poison of a snake into the wound. Others declared that she had had an adder smuggled to her in a basket of flowers and that she had let the adder bite her breast.

She lies buried today beside Mark Antony somewhere out in Egypt. Precisely where is still a mystery. If you go out to Alexandria and find her tomb, you will make a fortune and you will get your name flung in headlines across the front page of every important newspaper on earth.

GRETA GARBO
She painted her face with water colors

## THE GLAMOROUS GARBO USED TO WORK IN A BARBER SHOP

Two of the best known people in all the world both used to work in barber shops, one in London and the other in Stockholm. Both of them used to mix lather in shaving mugs and smear it on the faces of the customers, while the barbers honed their razors and got ready to mow down the whiskers. Both Greta Garbo and Charlie Chaplin once made their living in that fashion.

When Garbo came to America, people here had never heard of her. She couldn't even speak English. That was eight years ago. But today Garbo, at twenty-seven, is one of the most famous women on earth, more famous than all the bespangled kings and queens who have ever sat upon the Viking throne of her native Sweden during the past two hundred years.

As a child, Garbo was far from being a female prodigy. She disliked the humdrum of school, so she used to steal away frequently to the back porch of a theatre and stand tip-toe listening to a performance without buying a ticket. Tingling with excitement, she would rush home, paint her face with a child's set of water colors, and pretend she was Sarah Bernhardt parading in front of the footlights.

Her father died when she was fourteen, leaving the family in poverty. After working for a while in a barber shop, Greta finally got a job selling hats in a department store in Stockholm.

Then, one day, a trivial thing happened—a thing that altered her destiny and started her on the road to a fame far exceeding her most fantastic expectations. She posed for a hat advertisement. The ad boosted sales; so the store decided to make a moving picture advertisement of hats, and Greta posed as the model.

If a certain, keen-eyed, motion picture director hadn't seen that film, Garbo might still be selling hats today. This director was the first victim of the Garbo lure. She was only sixteen then, and he suggested that she study at a dramatic school.

It required the courage of a Viking to give up her regular salary and embark on such a financially precarious profession. In her thrifty Swedish soul, she still believes that leaving that hat store, with its dependable pay envelope, was the most perilous thing she ever did in her life.

One day, Maurice Stiller, the great Swedish director, sent to the dramatic school for a young girl to play a small part. Greta got the job. Her name then was Gustaffson. But Gustaffson isn't a poetical name. It hasn't glamour. It doesn't cling to the memory. So, with the wave of a magic wand, Greta Gustaffson was transformed into Greta Garbo.

Greta is one of the shyest and most mysterious women on earth. She is a mystery even to the people who work with her. For example, Wallace Beery has worked on the same lot with her for two years—and he has never even seen her. And more astonishing still is the fact that Wallace Beery played in the same picture with her without ever seeing her. The picture was *Grand Hotel*. They played in different scenes, and these scenes were made at different times.

Arthur Brisbane, the most famous editorial writer in America, recently went to Hollywood and said he wanted to see Greta Garbo making a picture. So he was taken out onto Garbo's set. But the Swedish Bird of Paradise refused to show herself while he was present. She said, "I read Mr. Brisbane's articles, and I admire him, but I can't act while he is looking at me."

When Garbo goes into the throes of an emotional scene, she often demands that even her director leave the set. And no one sees her but her camera man.

His name is William Daniels. He worked on her first picture in this country. In those days, she made amusing "breaks" in English, and everyone laughed at her—everyone except William Daniels. He had tact enough to realize that this strangely beautiful young girl was sensitive and ill-at-ease. So when the picture was finished, he congratulated her and said he hoped he might work with her again. She almost wept with gratitude.

When Garbo went to Europe, did the president of her company hear from her? No. He didn't even get a picture postcard. But Daniels, her camera man, got a cablegram.

The moment she is finished with one scene, she hides away, like a hunted deer, in a portable dressing room on the stage. She darts into this hiding place and refuses to come out again until she is called for another scene.

One policeman stands at the door of the sound stage, guarding her, and another policeman stands by the high fence which shuts off her set. It is easier to get in to see the President of the United States, or the King of England, than it is to see Greta Garbo.

Although she has millions of admirers, she has very few friends. She has a terrific inferiority complex. In spite of all her fame, she trembles when she is introduced to an important person. And she is one of the most lonesome women in the world. She eats her Christmas dinner all alone, in her big, silent house, with its massive furniture. Only two people come to that house as intimate friends. The telephone seldom rings. Laughter is rarely heard.

Not more than a few dozen people in America know where Greta Garbo lives. Even the people who live right next door to her don't realize that the great Garbo is just across the wall. She once took a house, paid three months' rent in advance, and lived in it only three days because a photographer had discovered her hiding place.

Garbo lives more simply than any other important picture star in the world. She drives about in a battered old car, of 1927 vintage. The old bus needs painting; and it is so ancient-looking that it is almost comical. She has only three servants. One is her chauffeur, another is her negro maid, and she has a cook. Her living expenses are about one hundred dollars a week, and her salary is $7,500 a week. She ought to be able to lay by an honest dollar now and then.

Her chauffeur, by the way, always carries a gun.

She loves animals, and she will rarely pass a dog or a horse without stopping to pet him and talk to him.

She keeps frogs and gold fish in her swimming pool. My friend, Homer Croy, tells me that when he met Garbo she was playing with a frog and the only thing she talked to him about was frogs.

Greta likes to go around in a sweater and sailor trousers. When she is off the screen, she uses no make-up whatever. She never rouges, nor paints her lips, nor dyes her finger nails. She has tiny freckles on both sides of her nose.

## ABOUT WELL KNOWN PEOPLE

You have heard the jokes about her feet. As a matter of fact, her feet are not large for her size. She is five feet, six inches tall, and wears a size seven, double A shoe. I am told that is an average size for a woman of her weight and height.

Her teeth are as sound as polished ivory. She has never once visited a dentist. "Applesauce" was the first English word she ever learned. She picked that up first because she heard it so frequently around the studios. And if you asked Greta Garbo today to describe Hollywood in one word, she would probably still say, "applesauce."

CROWN PRINCE RUDOLF
He died in bed—with his boots on

# THE PILLOWS OF THE CROWN PRINCE
# WERE STAINED WITH BLOOD

ON a cold, foggy morning, shortly before sunrise, in January 1889, three pistol shots rang out in the hunting lodge of Rudolf, the Crown Prince of the mighty Austro-Hungarian Empire.

Rudolf's friends, who had been spending the night under his roof, knocked and pounded excitedly on the door leading to the royal bedchamber. Hearing no response, they quickly pried the door off its hinges and dashed into the room.

The sight that greeted their eyes made them gasp with horror. The room was in wild disorder. Chairs were overturned, empty champagne bottles lay helter-skelter on the floor. The pillows on the bed were stained a brilliant red, and the walls were bespattered with blood. The Crown Prince Rudolf, fully dressed, even to his hunting boots, lay across the bed, with the top of his head blown off. Beside him, lay the nude body of the woman he loved. She had been killed by a bullet in her temple. The wound was covered by her luxuriant brown hair, which Rudolf had often caressed so tenderly. There wasn't a visible mark on her body. Beautiful as a Greek goddess, she was as lovely in death as she had been in life.

This tragedy occurred almost half a century ago in far off Austria; yet that murder—or suicide—is probably affecting your life right now, and has had a profound effect upon the history of the world.

The explanation is simple.

If the democratic Crown Prince Rudolf had lived, it is quite possible that he would have refused, in 1914, to join the forces of Austria with the German Kaiser, whom he despised. It is quite possible that Rudolf would have refused to fight against England, which he loved. And so, there might have been no world war and no depression affecting you now.

Did Rudolf shoot his sweetheart and then commit suicide? Or did some third party murder both of them? No one knows. Intrigued by this tragic romance, a score of people have written books about it—books in German and English and Italian. But the dark secret of that royal tragedy will probably never be solved.

Only two friends were in the hunting lodge when the shooting occurred. Prince Philip of Coburg and Count Hoyos, and they both thought it was suicide. They knew—almost everyone in Vienna knew—that Crown Prince Rudolf was unhappily married.

Eight years previously, he had married the golden-haired Princess Stephanie, daughter of the King of the Belgians. But he didn't love her and she didn't love him. The marriage had been forced upon them for political reasons. For years, they had been estranged. She seldom visited his apartments; and yet she was madly jealous of his attentions to other women.

Rudolf had traveled widely, spoke ten languages, had written books and was extremely popular. In fact, he was the toast of Vienna; the idol of an Empire.

In 1888, the year before his death, he met Baroness Marie Vetsera, a charming, vivacious young woman, with blood of the old Greeks coursing through her veins. She was nineteen; he was twenty-nine; and they fell romantically, ecstatically, in love.

The flaming love affair startled even the scandal-hardened drawing rooms of Vienna, and the rumblings of it reached the stern old Emperor, Franz Joseph. At first, he winked at the alliance, for he himself had never worn a spotless cloak of morality. But the flagrant affair persisted. It grew worse. It became a public scandal. All Vienna and Budapest gossiped about little else. So Franz Joseph called his son Rudolf to the palace and told him this wild, illicit love affair had to stop.

But Rudolf defied the old Emperor, swearing that he would never give up Marie. And Franz Joseph stormed and threatened and banged the table. But it availed nothing, for Marie meant more to Rudolf than honor and riches and the sparkling crown of the Hapsburgs. In fact, he wanted to renounce all claim to the throne, divorce his wife and marry Marie. But the old Emperor flew into another rage of denunciation.

So Rudolf and Marie often met secretly, after that, at his hunting lodge, nestling among the pine trees, thirty miles away from the prying eyes and wagging tongues of Vienna.

And there they had gone again on that fatal week in January, to steal a few happy days of love, when suddenly three pistol shots rang out—and altered the course of history.

On the morning of the tragedy, Rudolf was awakened by his valet at six-thirty o'clock, to go hunting. But his valet told him that the weather was foggy, and extremely cold; so Rudolf gave up the idea of hunting that day, ordered his carriage and said he would return to Vienna.

The valet was the last man who ever saw him alive, and he declared that the Prince was happy and smiling that morning. The valet was always positive that Rudolf and Marie had been murdered.

What possible motive could have prompted Rudolf to commit suicide? Few men on earth have ever had so much to live for. Stupendous wealth. Immense popularity. Youth. Love. Fame. And the throne of the Hapsburgs.

The old Emperor, anxious to hush up the affair, ordered the court physician to sign a statement saying that Rudolf had died of apoplexy. But the physician flatly refused.

Rudolf was buried with regal pomp and splendor among his Hapsburg ancestors, who had ruled Austria for six centuries. But the body of his sweetheart was tossed into a clothes basket and put in the butler's pantry at the hunting lodge, and left there unattended and unnoticed, for several days.

Finally, she was buried, at night, in a lonely monastery, deep in the heart of a dense pine forest.

The monks placed her body in a crude pine coffin made of rough slabs. The bark on the slabs caught on her dress as she was lowered into the box. The hat that she had worn so gayly as she came to her love tryst with Rudolf, was placed under her head for a pillow.

The mournful wind, sighing among the pine trees, was her only requiem.

# THEY TRIED TO SHOOT MARCONI FOR INVENTING RADIO

It was my good fortune, not long ago, to spend an hour with a man who has had a profound effect on your life. He has changed the world in which you live. He has made it possible for you to send a message around the earth in one seventh of a second. He has also made it possible for you to sit in your home, turn a dial on your radio, and hear the President speak from the White House, or listen to some famous orchestra playing the enchanting strains of the "Blue Danube."

We always think of Marconi as an Italian. And his father *was* Italian; but his mother was Irish and her home was in London. His Irish blood has given him light hair and blue eyes and he looks far more like a Britisher than an Italian. He speaks perfect English, but with a slight London accent. And he wears a monacle, British-fashion, over his left eye—he unfortunately lost the use of his right eye in an automobile accident twenty years ago.

As I sat talking to this soft-spoken, modest, unassuming man, it was hard for me to realize that I was in the presence of one of the most distinguished men on earth. Years ago, when I was a little boy, back in Missouri, I had read of a great scientist over in Italy who had discovered wireless telegraphy; and then, one day in 1920, Lowell Thomas and I went to lunch in a restaurant in London where it was possible to hear a new-fangled contraption called a radio.

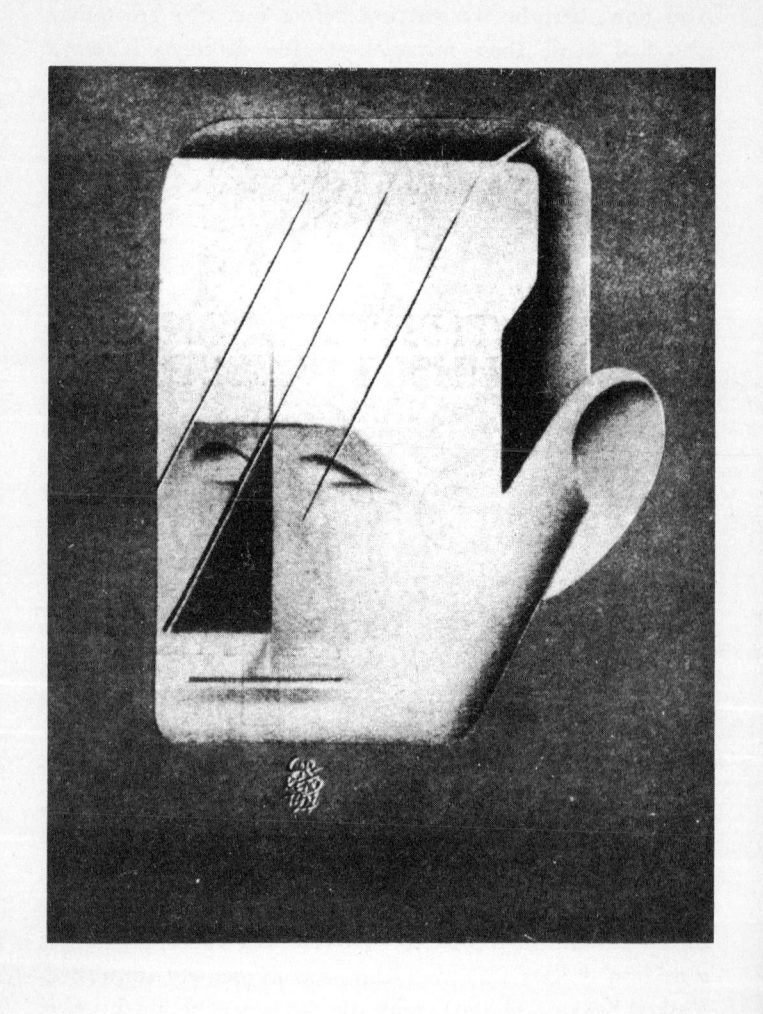

MARCONI
With his first $250,000 he went out and bought a bicycle

## ABOUT WELL KNOWN PEOPLE

And now, here he was, sitting before me, this great man who had made these miracles possible. It seemed almost like a dream.

I asked him how he first came to be interested in experimenting with radio, and he said it was largely because, as a young man, he wanted to do some sort of work that would enable him to travel all over the earth. He told me that he had often traveled with his mother, from their home in Italy, to visit her people in London; and as he crossed France and sat looking out of the train window, there flashed before his eyes glacier-clad mountains, turbulent rivers and chateaux glamorous with romance; so even then, in his childhood, there was born in Marconi an urge, a veritable passion, for travel. And he told me that he felt, by experimenting with electrical waves and devoting his life to wireless telegraphy, he would have an opportunity to get out under the sky and travel to far-off lands. He said he could never have stood the confinement of working in some small shop. Marconi now does almost all his work aboard his yacht, which is a floating laboratory. He still loves to travel, and he has crossed the Atlantic Ocean eighty-seven times.

While he was still a very young man, Marconi was able to send wireless messages across the room in his own home; then, finally, he sent messages a distance of two miles. He was greatly excited. His father told him he was wasting his time; but a few years later, young Marconi sold some of his patents to the British government for a quarter of a million dollars and his father was immensely impressed. I asked Senator Marconi what he did when he got his first $250,000 and he said he went out and bought a bicycle and then went back to work again as usual. To him, the excitement of his experiments was more alluring than anything money could buy.

In 1901, Marconi believed that the great dream of his life was about to come true; so he rushed across the Atlantic Ocean, confidently expecting that he would be able to receive messages in America from his sending station in England.

Landing in Newfoundland, Marconi sent up a kite to act as an aerial—a kite made of bamboo and silk. But the wind ripped the frail kite to shreds. Then he sent up a balloon; and the wind smashed the balloon and hurled it into the ocean. Finally, he got a kite that would stay up; and he listened—listened for hours, waiting breathlessly for the signals that were supposed to come from his station in Cornwall, England. But none came; there wasn't a sound. Tragically disappointed, he believed that his experiment was a failure, that the great dream of his life had been blasted.

Then, suddenly, he heard a faint click. Then another. Then another. Yes, that was it. There it was: the signal they had agreed upon. The three dots which stood for the letter S in the alphabet used by telegraph operators. Flushed with excitement, Marconi knew that his achievement was big with history. He longed to rush out and shout the news from the housetops. But should he? No. He feared people wouldn't believe him; so for forty-eight hours he shared his secret with no one. Then, gathering courage, he cabled the facts to London. They created a sensation. Newspapers on five continents featured the story; and it set the scientific world seething with excitement. Man, triumphing once more over time and space, trembled on the threshold of a new era. Wireless telegraphy had been born; and it was destined to transform the world for you and me.

And how old was Marconi when he did all this? Only twenty-seven. Immediately, he began getting letters from cranks. These fanatics complained bitterly because they imagined that his electrical waves were passing through their bodies, destroying their nerves and making it impossible for them to sleep.

Several of these cranks threatened to kill Marconi. One of them—a German—said he was coming to London to shoot him. His letter was turned over to Scotland Yard; and the British Government wouldn't let him land in England.

I asked Senator Marconi how long it would be before you and I could have good, practical television sets in our homes. He said probably in about ten years, maybe sooner; so it won't be long now before we will be sitting in front of our fireplaces, watching a fashion show in Paris, or a football game in California.

**CATHERINE THE GREAT OF RUSSIA**
Her name wasn't Catherine; she wasn't Russian; her greatness
is hotly disputed

## SHE RULED AN EMPIRE, MARRIED AN IMBECILE, AND HAD A SCORE OF LOVERS

Catherine the Great was the most famous Empress that ever sat upon the glittering throne of Russia.

Yet her real name was not Catherine. And she was not Russian. And some historians don't even think she was great.

When she came to Russia, she was a nobody—a little poverty-stricken German princess, who had been reared like a ragamuffin. She arrived in Russia, friendless and penniless, and with only three dresses to her name. Yet she managed to marry the Grand Duke Peter, the heir to the throne of all the Russias. But Peter didn't amount to much. He was a driveling imbecile. His face was pitted and marked with the ravages of small-pox, and he used to go to bed with his boots on. Even after he became Czar, he got drunk with his own servants, took a whip and beat his soldiers with his own hands, and lay on the floor, for hours at a time, playing with wax dolls dressed in military uniform.

Catherine had several children; but this half-witted husband of hers refused to recognize any of them because he claimed they weren't his.

He insulted Catherine in public before hundreds of guests, called her names that I don't dare repeat and threatened to divorce her; and he also threatened to shut her up in a convent for life.

He despised her, and she loathed him. So she staged a revolt, kicked him off the throne, and had one of her lovers put arsenic in his vodka.

But he was so tough that even arsenic couldn't kill him; so Catherine's lover knocked him down and choked him to death by thrusting a napkin down his throat.

Then, for thirty-four years after that, Catherine ruled one of the greatest empires on earth—ruled over a land inhabited by fifty different races, and she called it her "Little Household." She never married again; but she wasn't exactly lonesome. For scores, yea, perhaps hundreds of different lovers, danced in the ballroom of her warm and romantic heart. Yet she was so strict with her grandsons that she made them stop studying botany because they asked questions about the reproduction of plants.

She supported her lovers in regal splendor and squandered on them five hundred million dollars. Even though some of them hadn't the least bit of ability, nevertheless she made them generals in the army. She made them generals and plutocrats and premiers. She conquered Poland and made one of her lovers King of Poland. He didn't want to be a king; but she was tired of him and wanted to get rid of him so she made him a king anyway. Later on, she ruined him, and brought his gilded throne back to Russia and used it in her bath room.

One of her favorites was Gregory Orloff, a handsome army officer who had the physique of a Greek god, and the technique of a cave-man. He used to take his fists and beat the Empress black and blue. Then he would tire of her and desert her for weeks at a time, and go about kissing every pretty servant girl in the palace. But Catherine was nothing if she wasn't broad-minded, so she forgave her handsome Orloff and adored him and showered titles upon him and presented him with palaces and serfs by the thousands. Finally, he ran off with a chit of a girl and went mad.

Then Catherine the Great fell in love with an ugly giant, bearing the name of Potemkin. Potemkin only had one eye. He had lost the other one in a tavern brawl.

Although Potemkin lived in a palace glittering with all the splendor and riches of Asia, he went about with nothing but house slippers on his bare feet. His hair was uncombed; and he always needed a bath. He chewed his finger nails; and he ate raw onions and garlic. But Potemkin was a tornado of physical energy, and the mere touch of his hand filled Catherine with a vast and tender happiness. She called him her "golden pheasant," her "pigeon," her "bow-wow."

Her "bow-wow" was one of the greatest generals Russia ever had; and yet he was afraid of the noise of guns and trembled like a school girl whenever a cannon was fired.

Although Catherine was the richest woman in the world, she ate only two meals a day; and almost anyone in America of modest income enjoys better cooked food than Catherine the Great often had. She had her dinners served on plates of gold; yet if the cook burned the meat, she merely laughed and ate it just the same.

Although one of the greatest voluptuaries that ever lived, yet she never drank wine nor an alcoholic liquor. But she did drink sweet currant juice, and she also drank five cups of strong coffee every morning. A whole pound of coffee was used to make those five cups.

She was surrounded by hundreds of servants; yet she

often built her own fires. She never smoked in her life; but she used bushels of snuff. Her clothes were sprinkled with it, and were so saturated with the smell of it that she reeked from afar.

Tall and straight as a grenadier, she took great pride in her imperial carriage and stretched her neck to make herself appear taller—though when she was a child, her body was so twisted and deformed that, for years, she had to wear a strait-jacket, night and day.

She had the skull formation of a child of six. She was twenty-six years old before the bones of her skull grew together, and she was tortured incessantly by excruciating headaches.

Proud and haughty, she wouldn't even open a letter unless it was addressed to her as "Imperial Majesty," and she once had a man's nose cut off because he got drunk and claimed he was her husband.

As Catherine grew older, she waxed enormously fat—so fat her feet would no longer support her elephantine weight, and she had to be pushed about in a wheel chair.

But toothless and huge as she was, the winds of spring still stirred in her romantic soul; so she fell in love again—this time with a chap young enough to be her grandson. And during the last years of her reign, this vain, addlepated gigolo ruled Russia like a Czar.

# THE PUNCTUAL NAPOLEON KEPT HER WAITING TWO HOURS AT THE ALTAR

THIS is the story of a poor girl who was born in a fishing village down in the West Indies and who lived in bare, dingy rooms over a sugar refinery; the story of a girl who married the most famous man in all history.

Her name was Marie Joseph Rose Tasher La Pagerie, but she is usually called "Josephine."

Josephine was six years older than Napoleon. When they first met, she was thirty-three and he was only twenty-seven. She was not good looking; she had bad teeth and two half-grown children, and she was in debt—deeply in debt. In fact, she was only two jumps ahead of the sheriff. So we must admit she started with severe handicaps. But she had one enormous asset: she knew how to handle men. She was a widow and she had had experience.

When the French revolutionists cut off the head of her first husband, Josephine found herself without means of support; and she did what most sensible widows do; she began looking about for a husband.

One of her friends told her about Napoleon. He hadn't become famous yet, and he didn't have any money. The fact is, he had just returned from a war and the only thing he had brought back with him was the itch, and he had shaved his head to get rid of that.

But Josephine's friends told her that Napoleon was go-

**JOSEPHINE**
She had bad teeth, two children, and the sheriff in pursuit

ing to make a name for himself. And so Josephine, being human, wanted to meet him.

But how? She figured out a clever way to do it. She sent her young son, who was twelve years old, to ask Napoleon if he might have the sword of his (the boy's) dead father. Naturally, Napoleon said yes; and the next day Josephine powdered her nose and went to thank Napoleon, with tears in her eyes for his great kindness.

Napoleon was immensely impressed by Josephine's personality and by her extraordinary charm. He realized that she was above him, socially; so when she invited him to her house for tea, he was flattered. And when he came to tea, she told him he was going to be one of the greatest generals in all history. . . . Three months later, their engagement was announced.

Napoleon had a veritable passion for always being on time. His motto was "Time is everything," and he once said, "I may lose battles, but no one will ever see me lose minutes;" and yet he was two hours late for his own wedding! The Justice of the Peace who was waiting to marry them got so tired that he yawned and fell asleep before Napoleon arrived.

Forty-eight hours after his marriage, Napoleon set out to wage a new war in Italy. His army was a hungry, ragged affair; yet he fought a brilliant campaign that electrified the continent. Europe hadn't seen such fighting in a thousand years.

And the amazing part of it all is that, even on the battlefields, Napoleon found time to write Josephine a letter every day. And what letters! Ardent, flaming, tempestous affairs! In 1933, eight of Napoleon's love letters to Josephine were sold at public auction in London for

$20,000. I have read them and believe that they are worth twenty thousand dollars—even in 1933. For example:

*My dear Josephine:*

*You have inspired me with a love which has taken away my reason—I can't eat. I can't sleep. I don't care for my friends. I don't care for glory; I value victory only because it pleases you. If it weren't for that, I should leave the army and hurry back to Paris to fling myself at your feet.*

*You have inspired me with a limitless love; you have filled me with an intoxicating frenzy. Never an hour passes without my looking at your portrait, and never an hour passes without my covering it with kisses.*

And that is tame in comparison to some of the things he wrote. Most women would give their right arm for letters like that. But Josephine didn't seem to care for them. She was having a flirtation with another man and she drove Napoleon almost frantic because she didn't even bother to answer his letters.

Finally, he got fed up with her indifference and, while he was fighting in Egypt, he invited a blonde to have tea with him. And Josephine heard about it way off in Paris!

When Napoleon returned to France, there was the devil to pay—as there usually is in such cases. She told him what she thought and he told her what he thought; and it ended by Napoleon locking Josephine out of his room.

Then there were family troubles. Josephine was better bred than Napoleon's sisters and that made them jealous and envious. They thought she was snubbing them, and that made them hopping mad. They swore to high Heaven that they would get even with her. They began poking

# ABOUT WELL KNOWN PEOPLE

fun at her and calling her the "old woman" and telling Napoleon that he ought to divorce his "fat, old wife" and marry a younger woman.

But talk as much as they might, they couldn't kill Napoleon's love for Josephine. Nothing could do that. Nothing.

However, he did decide to divorce her, and he decided to do it for one reason only: he wanted a wife who could bear him a son. It broke his heart to do it and he wept as he signed the divorce papers; and for three days after that, he sat in his palace, staring into space, brooding, and refusing to see anybody, or do anything. Shortly after the divorce, Napoleon married Marie Louise, of Austria.

The curious part of it is that Marie Louise, like all Austrians, had been brought up to despise Napoleon; and she prayed to Almighty God that she wouldn't have to marry him. But her father insisted that she do it for political reasons; and so she married him, by proxy, before she ever even saw him. But she didn't care for him; and when he began to lose battles, she deserted him, and even taught his own son to hate him.

Napoleon's first love and last love, and only real love, was Josephine. And after she died, he visited her grave and wept, saying,

"My darling Josephine, at least she would never have deserted me."

The last word that Napoleon ever spoke on this earth was the word "Josephine."

*Courtesy of The New Yorker*
**ORVILLE WRIGHT**
He expected the darn thing to work, and it did

## HE CHANGED THE WORLD'S HISTORY
## BUT GOT NO THRILL OUT OF IT

LESS than forty years ago, a trivial event occurred out in Ohio. At least, it seemed trivial at the time; but we know now that this event has influenced your life and that it is going to have a mighty influence on the lives of your children, and your children's children.

On that momentous day, Orville Wright walked into a library, in Dayton, Ohio, and picked up a book. This book told the story of a German by the name of Lilienthal who was able to fly in a glider or huge kite. To be sure, Lilienthal didn't use an engine, but he did fly. Orville Wright sat up that night, until long past midnight, fascinated with the story of this significant achievement. He aroused the enthusiasm of his brother, Wilbur; and the Wright brothers started out on a career that was to end in the invention of the airplane and make their names immortal.

Neither of them had much education. They never finished high school. But they had something far more important than a college diploma. They had resourcefulness and ambition. Years before, when they were mere boys, they had gone out into the country and picked up the bones of dead cows and horses and sold them to a fertilizer factory. Then they gathered up scraps of iron and sold them to a junk dealer. Later, they built a printing press and tried to publish a daily paper, but it failed. Then they started a little shop where they sold and repaired bicycles.

But no matter what they did for a living, they were always dreaming about flying. On Sunday afternoons, they would lie for hours on their backs, on a sunny hillside, watching the buzzards circling over head and the chicken hawks soaring aloft on rising currents of air.

Building a wind tunnel in their bicycle shop, they began experimenting with the force of air on wings; and they were constantly fiddling with kites. Finally, they built a huge kite or glider and took it down to Kill Devil Hill at Kitty Hawk, North Carolina. They went to Kitty Hawk because a strong, salty wind is always sweeping in there from the sea and the ground there is always soft with billowy sand.

For years, they experimented with gliders; and then they put a home-made engine in one of their gliders and transformed it into a flying machine. They made the date, December 17th, 1903, forever memorable by achieving the first flight in the annals of human history. They flipped a half-dollar to see who would be the first to go up. Heads turned up and Orville won. It was a bitter, sunless day. A biting wind whipped up the ice floes along the shore at Kitty Hawk; and the angry surf pounded and boomed on the beach half a mile away. Five men, tinkering with the plane, slapped their arms and danced and jumped to keep warm. But cold as it was, Orville wouldn't wear even an overcoat when he mounted the plane because of the additional weight.

At exactly thirty-five minutes past ten o'clock, Orville Wright climbed onto the roaring craft, stretched out on his stomach, pulled the release, and the strange machine rose, snorting and coughing, into the air, with flames

## ABOUT WELL KNOWN PEOPLE

belching from the open exhaust. The machine plunged up and down uncertainly for twelve historic seconds; and then lighted on the ground only one hundred feet away.

It was a tremendous event. It was one of the turning points in the history of civilization. At last, the great dream of the ages had come true. For the first time, a man had shaken off the shackles of earth and soared up toward the stars.

Yet Orville Wright said he didn't get any thrill out of it at all. He said he expected the darn thing to work, and it did. That was all. He said he never cared much about flying, and that the only thrill he ever did get out of aviation was one night, when he lay awake in bed, as a boy, and dreamed about the possibility of flying.

And here is a strange thing:

Orville Wright, the first man who ever flew, doesn't have a license to fly now, he has not been up in an airplane since 1918, and he hasn't piloted a plane since 1914.

Why? Because back in 1908, he was piloting a plane at Fort Myers, Virginia. Something snapped. The plane crashed to the earth. The observer was killed; but Orville Wright escaped with an injured spine. But the injury was so severe, the pain was so excruciating that, even to this day, Orville Wright suffers agony when he travels. To be sure, he can walk all right; but he can't bear the slightest bit of a jar.

He is a shy man, and to him the hue and cry of publicity is most unwelcome. He won't write the story of his life. He won't have his picture taken, and he doesn't like to talk to reporters. His brother, Wilbur, who died in 1912, once said, "The only birds that talk are parrots, and they don't fly very high."

Both the Wright brothers were modest and self-effacing. One day, Wilbur reached into his pocket for a handkerchief, and a red ribbon fell onto the floor. His sister asked him what it was, and he said, nonchalantly, "Oh! That! I forgot to tell you. That's the ribbon of the Legion of Honor that the French Government gave me this afternoon."

Orville and Wilbur Wright, nourished on the precepts of an old-fashioned religion, always declined to fly on Sunday. On one occasion, the King of Spain asked to be taken up on a Sunday, but, clinging to the dictates of their conscience, they refused the royal command.

Neither of the Wright brothers ever married. Their father once said that the boys couldn't afford both wives and a flying machine. So they chose the flying machine.

## HE MADE A FORTUNE OUT OF A MOUSE AND THREE PIGS

EIGHT years ago, Walt Disney, the man who created Mickey Mouse and the Three Little Pigs, was almost unknown. Today, he is one of the most famous men in America for his age, which is thirty two.

The current edition of *Who's Who in Great Britain* lists Walt Disney among the great of the world, and devotes more space to him than is given to the charming Prince of Wales.

Nine years ago, Walt Disney was hard pressed to get enough to eat. Today, he is known and loved all the way from the tea fields of Ceylon to the fishing villages of the frozen North. Even the Eskimos, way up near the Arctic Circle, became so enthusiastic over the Mickey Mouse films that they saw in Juneau, Alaska, that they formed a Mickey Mouse Club which meets in an igloo.

Nine years ago, Walt Disney was "broke." Today, he is very wealthy. He could swank about in a glittering Rolls Royce, if he wanted to; but instead, he uses an old car that he bought second-hand. He takes all of his profits and plows them back into his business. He says that making better pictures interests him far more than piling up millions.

Walt Disney used to live in Kansas City, and he was ambitious to be an artist; so, one day, he went to the *Kansas City Star* to get a job. The editor examined his

WALT DISNEY
Some of his fans met in an igloo

## ABOUT WELL KNOWN PEOPLE

drawings, told him he didn't have any real talent, discouraged him, and sent him away with a broken heart.

Finally, he got a poorly paid job making drawings for churches. He couldn't afford to rent an office, so he had to use his father's garage for his studio. He thought at the time that it was hardship, but he realizes now that, working amidst the grease and gasoline smells of that garage, gave him an idea that was worth a million dollars.

It happened in this way: One day, a mouse started playing on the floor of the wooden garage. Disney stopped and looked at him; and then went into the house and got some crumbs and fed him.

As the days went by, that mouse became so friendly that he would climb up on top of Disney's drawing board.

Disney finally went out to Hollywood and started a series of animated cartoons called "Oswald the Rabbit," but that was a flat failure. So again he soon found himself without money and without a job.

One day, he was sitting in a rooming house, trying to think up an idea, when suddenly there popped into his mind the mouse who used to climb up on his drawing board back in the Kansas City garage.

Instantly, he started to sketch a mouse—and that's how Mickey Mouse was born. That mouse in Kansas City, long since dead and gone, was the great-grandfather of the most famous motion picture actor the world has ever known. Mickey Mouse gets more fan letters than any other actor in the films; and he frolics across the screen in more different countries than any other actor in the world.

Walt Disney goes out to the Zoo every week to study the animals and the sounds they make, for he himself makes the mouse noises in his Mickey pictures; and he also makes the noises of most of the other animals.

Disney never makes the actual drawings that go into his pictures; neither does he write the words, nor compose the music.

He has a staff of one hundred and thirty-four assistants looking after details like that.

Walt Disney himself devotes all of his time to thinking up ideas for pictures; and when he gets an idea, he discusses it with his staff of twelve assistants in the story department. One day, about two years ago, he suggested to his staff that they make a picture out of a nursery story that his mother had read to him as a child—the story of the Three Little Pigs and the Big, Bad Wolf.

His assistants shook their heads, and turned down their thumbs. Disney says he tried to forget about the idea; but he simply couldn't. However, every time he suggested it, his staff warned him it would be a "flop."

Finally, the staff said "All right. Let's go ahead with it," but they didn't have much faith in it.

It takes ninety days to make a Mickey Mouse film; but they didn't propose to waste that much time on Three Little Pigs, so they rushed it out in sixty days. No one in the studio thought it would amount to much. Yet it took the country by storm.

It was a sensational success. Everyone, from the cotton fields of Georgia to the apple orchards of Oregon, was soon singing "Who's Afraid of the Big Bad Wolf, the Big Bad Wolf, the Big Bad Wolf?"

Mr. Disney informs me that some theatres recalled the picture seven different times. It is the greatest success that has ever been known in the history of animated cartoons.

It has been estimated that the Three Little Pigs would

# ABOUT WELL KNOWN PEOPLE

pile up three million dollars in profit; but Mr. Disney says it will only net him about $125,000 and that it will take two years to earn that.

However, these cartoon pictures have a long life. There are audiences somewhere this very minute looking at Mickey Mouse pictures that were made eight years ago.

Walt Disney believes the secret of success lies in being in love with your work. He says the idea of merely making money doesn't appeal to him. His work is the real thrill and adventure of his existence.

He plays baseball every day at noon, and he occasionally plays polo with Will Rogers; but he says he gets more of a real thrill out of his work than he does out of his play.

The tune of "Who's Afraid of the Big Bad Wolf" was the first song hit that ever came from an animated cartoon. One of Disney's men, Frank Churchill, wrote the tune in five minutes on the back of an envelope. After it made a hit, he immediately received offers from five other movie companies.

**NICHOLAS II**
Publicly he was pictured as a monster; privately, he was a meek, kindly man who didn't complain

## HE RULED ONE SIXTH OF THE WORLD— AND WAS SHOT IN A DIRTY CELLAR

ONE of the richest men that Europe ever knew, and one of the most famous men in all the world, was worth, when he died, about fifty million dollars in land, eighty million dollars in diamonds and pearls and rubies, and possessed an income of a million dollars a month or *Twenty-four Dollars a Second*.

Yet, a little after midnight, on July 16, 1918, he and his family were herded into a dirty cellar, full of cobwebs, and shot. The story of their assassination is one of the most dramatic tales in the annals of history.

This man was Nicholas II, the last Czar of Russia—the man who, for almost a quarter of a century, ruled with an iron hand over one-sixth of all the land on earth.

In 1917, after almost three years of futile slaughter, his armies revolted and refused to fight any longer, and so, a few minutes before midnight, on March 14, 1917, a committee of generals met the Czar of Russia in the drawing room of his private train and told him he would have to renounce his power and give up his throne.

He was so shocked that he swayed from side to side and turned deathly pale. The committee was afraid that he would actually faint and fall to the floor.

He went to his bed, but he found it impossible to sleep. So he got up and spent the rest of the night reading one of Shakespeare's great plays, *Julius Caesar*.

The next morning, promptly at 11:15, he signed his abdication with an ordinary lead pencil and said, "Thank God. I can now do what I have always wanted to do. I can go to my home in Crimea and raise flowers."

The Czar and his family spent the last months of their lives in two rooms of an old house on the outskirts of a town at the foot of the Ural Mountains. Held there as prisoners by the revolutionists, they were forced to eat like peasants. They were allowed no sugar, no coffee, no cream, no salt and no butter. They had nothing to eat except a coarse, black bread and a thick, vegetable soup twice a day.

The windows of the house were painted over so that they couldn't see out and they were not allowed to open the windows. One day, the youngest princess, Anastasia, opened a window for a breath of air and a soldier fired at her. They were allowed to walk in a little garden for five minutes each day. The little Czarevitch was too ill to walk; and so his father carried the boy in his arms.

The soldiers who were guarding them went around half-clothed, addressed indecent remarks to the young daughters of the Czar and sang filthy songs under their windows at night. One day, one of the guards snatched a pocketbook from the Empress and took away her money, saying: "You won't need money any longer."

The Czar himself was a meek, kindly man and he didn't complain. But his wife was very domineering and she complained bitterly and incessantly, and vowed to high Heaven that some day she would have her revenge on these beasts.

Shortly after midnight, on the evening of July 16, 1918, the captain of the guards awakened the Czar and his family and told them that rioting had broken out in the town

# ABOUT WELL KNOWN PEOPLE 63

and that they must dress quickly and go down to the cellar and wait there until automobiles came to take them to a place of safety. When the Empress reached the cellar, she was trembling with fear and she was unable to stand, so a chair had to be brought for her and she sat down, holding her little sick boy on her lap.

Presently the soldiers rushed down into the cellar and shouted: "Your friends have tried to save you but they didn't succeed and we are going to kill you."

Quickly a soldier fired point blank at the Czar and shot him through the heart. The instant he fell, the soldiers began shooting at the women; but the soldiers were so excited that their shots went wild and they fired again and again, while the helpless women ran back and forth, screaming and hiding behind one another and trying to shield themselves with feather pillows.

But the guards succeeded not only in shooting the women, but they stabbed them with bayonets. A few minutes later, the only sound in this tragic cellar was the frantic barking of a little dog who ran around over the dead bodies, trying to find his mistress. One of the soldiers stuck his bayonet through the little dog. The soldiers then cut the royal bodies into pieces, soaked them in gasoline, burned, and threw the charred remains down into the pit of an old iron mine.

A few days later, the soldiers poked about in the ashes where the bodies had been burned and found many precious stones, for the Empress and her daughters had hidden diamonds and rubies in the hems of their dresses.

This assassination, it should be said, was not an official act of the newly-formed Russian government. The Soviet government, in fact, arrested a number of revolutionists, tried them for the murder of the Czar, and shot five of them. The assassination of the royal family was the act of a few blood-thirsty revolutionists who took orders from no one.

The charred remains of the royal family are now buried in Paris, and the American flag helped to take them there. It happened in this way: In January, 1920, the American Consul General in Siberia, at the request of a friend, took a rough wooden box, tied with a rope, across Siberia and delivered it to the British High Commission at Harbin. The American Consul didn't know what was in the box and he didn't care. The train was cold and he used to kick his feet against the box to get them warm. When he arrived at Harbin, he was amazed to learn that the box contained the burned and mutilated remains of the dead Czar and his family. The box was sent to Shanghai and then to Paris. It was opened in Paris; and in it, among other things, was found a finger of the Empress with her wedding ring still on it.

The Czar was very fond of reading Shakespeare and he must have read these words often: "They that stand high have many winds to shake them; and if they fall, they dash themselves to pieces."

# THE WORLD'S BEST KNOWN MAN CARRIES FALSE TEETH IN HIS LOIN CLOTH

EVERY so often, out in India, a little, brown man, wearing a loin cloth, lays himself down on a cot, refuses to eat, and threatens to fast until he dies. Then newspapers all over the world feature the story because Mahatma Gandhi is one of the leading figures of this generation.

Reckoned in terms of money, Gandhi is a poor man. If he sold all his earthly possessions, they probably would not bring seventy-five cents; yet he is more powerful than any millionaire on earth.

Physically, he is weak; and he refuses to use force or violence; yet his teachings and his spiritual influence are more potent and powerful than a hundred battleships of England.

One person out of every six on earth lives in India. And for centuries, these people of India have been asleep; now this little, frail man, who weighs less than a hundred pounds, is arousing India to a sense of its own gigantic power! He is instituting reforms that may have far-reaching effects on the history of the world.

There are many curious things about Gandhi. For example, he has a set of false teeth, which he carries in a fold of his loin cloth. He puts them in his mouth only when he wants to eat. After his meal, he takes them out, washes them and puts them back in his loin cloth again.

He speaks English with an Irish accent, for one of his

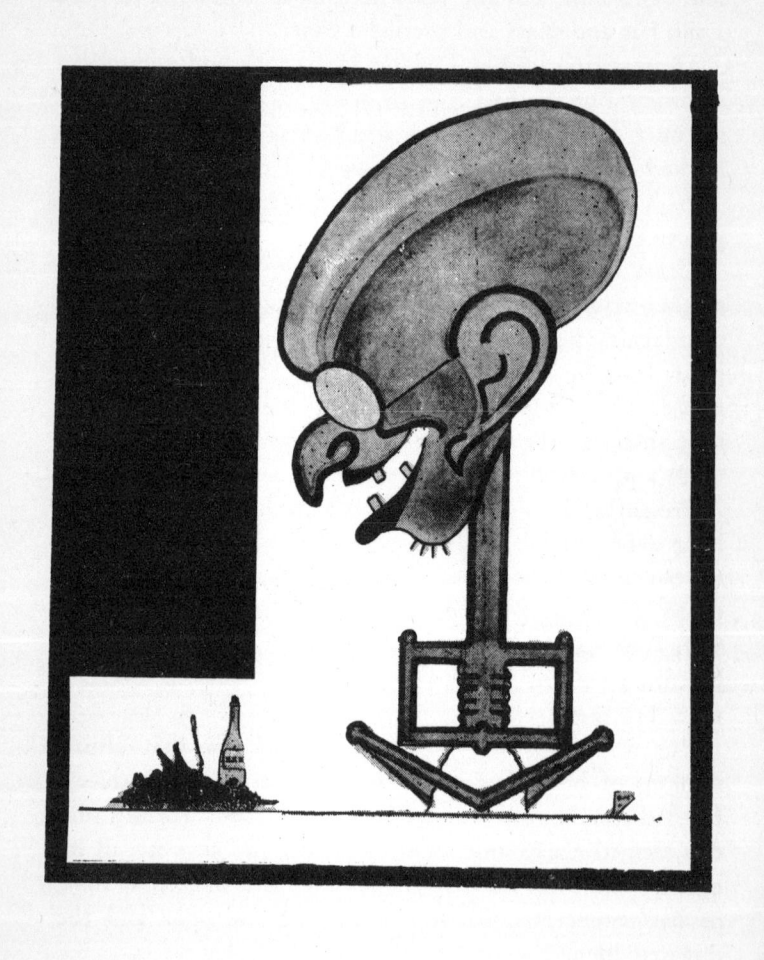

**MAHATMA GANDHI**
When he refuses to eat, editors yell for headlines

## ABOUT WELL KNOWN PEOPLE

first teachers was an Irishman. He wears nothing but a loin cloth now, but for years he lived in London and wore a silk hat and spats and carried a cane.

He was educated at London University and became an attorney. But the first time he attempted to make a speech in court, his knees trembled, and he was so frightened that he had to sit down in confusion and defeat.

As a lawyer in London, he got nowhere at all. He was practically a failure there.

Years before, when he first came to England, his Irish teacher made him copy the Sermon on the Mount, over and over again, purely as an exercise in English. Hour after hour, Gandhi wrote "Blessed are the meek, for they shall inherit the earth. . . . Blessed are the peacemakers for they shall be called the children of God," and these words made a profound impression on him.

Presently, he was sent to South Africa to collect some huge debts; and he tried to apply there the philosophy of the Sermon on the Mount. And it worked. Clients flocked to M. H. Gandhi because he settled their claims peacefully out of court and saved them time and expense. Gandhi soon had an income of fifteen thousand dollars a year. The meek was inheriting the earth.

But was he happy? No. Because he knew that untold millions of his fellow countrymen were living in misery. He had seen thousands die of starvation, and worldly success seemed cheap and unimportant. So he gave up all his money, and took the vow of poverty, and since that time, he has consecrated his life to helping the poor and the downtrodden. . . .

Today, one tenth of the population of India—more people than live in the United States, west of the Mississippi

River—are hungry and half-starved. Their condition is so hopeless that Gandhi is pleading with them to cease bringing children into a world filled with so much misery and want.

Gandhi experimented with diets to see how cheaply he could live and remain healthy. He now lives principally on fruit and goats' milk and olive oil.

Gandhi has been greatly influenced by the teachings of an American by the name of David Thoreau. Thoreau was graduated from Harvard University ninety years ago, and then spent twenty-eight dollars building a cabin for himself on the lonely shores of Walden Pond, in Massachusetts. He lived there like a hermit, and refused to pay taxes; so he was thrown into jail. He then wrote a book on Civil Disobedience, saying that no one ought to pay taxes. People didn't pay the slightest attention to his book then; but, seventy-five years later, Gandhi read that book, away out in India, and decided to use Thoreau's tactics. He felt that England had not kept her promise to give India self-government; so, in order to punish England, Gandhi urged the people of India to go to jail rather than pay taxes, and he also urged his followers to boycott English goods. When the British placed a tax on salt, Gandhi led his followers to the sea and they made their own salt.

India has about 60,000,000 people who, according to the Hindu religion, are forever branded as untouchables. What does that mean? Just this: take yourself, for example. Suppose you lived in India and your ancestors, two thousand years ago, had been branded as untouchables by the Hindu religion. That would mean that you too would be an untouchable today. Your soul would be condemned to suffer for the sins it had committed in some former life;

## ABOUT WELL KNOWN PEOPLE

and you would not be permitted to drink the water that comes from a village well. You would have to go and drink from some dirty wayside stream. You would be regarded as so loathsome that you would not dare enter a grocery store. You would have to stand outside, at a respectful distance, and have the food flung at you.

You couldn't enter a court of justice. You couldn't attend school. You couldn't even walk within five hundred feet of a public road. And, if even your shadow fell on food, it would be regarded as unfit to eat and would be destroyed.

Remember that there are 60,000,000 of these untouchables—half as many as the entire population of the United States. Their condition is the most pathetic and tragic thing in the world today, and Gandhi is devoting his life now to fighting for their rights. He has even adopted a little untouchable girl and is bringing her up as his own daughter.

Millions regard Mahatma Gandhi as a saint. Others believe that he is the reincarnation of a Hindu god. In a world filled with sordid greed and selfishness, I, for one, feel like standing with bowed head before this man who is seeking nothing for himself but is willing to die in order that others may live.

*Courtesy of G. P. Putnam Sons*
ADMIRAL RICHARD BYRD
At the age of twelve, he began to toughen himself for the Arctic

## THE NAVY COULDN'T USE HIM BUT HE IS NOW OUR MOST FAMOUS ADMIRAL

IN 1900, a little boy down in Winchester, Virginia, was keeping a diary. He had been inspired by the stories of Admiral Peary's heroic struggles to reach the North Pole; so in the autumn of 1900, this little twelve-year-old boy wrote in his diary, "I have decided to be the first man to reach the North Pole." And he immediately began preparing himself for that Spartan adventure. He detested cold weather, so he started to toughen himself by wearing light underwear and no overcoat.

Many years later, the boy who wrote that decision in his diary actually did reach the pole. In fact, he was the first man ever to fly over the North Pole, and he was also the first man ever to fly over the South Pole. His name, of course, is Richard Evelyn Byrd.

Commander Byrd declares that the mighty ice fields in the South Polar regions are slowly receding, and he believes that, some day, millions of acres of land, now smothered beneath slow, grinding glaciers, may prove to be extremely valuable; and so he is determined to plant the Stars and Stripes on that land and claim it forever in the name of the government of the United States. Commander Byrd is probably right. I have found coal deposits myself within 600 miles of the North Pole; and most geologists believe that fabulously wealthy coal deposits, and perhaps oil fields, exist near the South Pole.

Byrd's life is an inspiring illustration of a boy who had an undying ambition to do big things and who did them in spite of innumerable obstacles.

First, he wanted to travel and see strange lands. And by the time he was fourteen years of age, he had traveled all the way around the world—and he had done it all by himself. He came back home, and went to college; and in college, he devoted a lot of time to boxing, wrestling and football. In doing so, he broke a bone in his foot, crushed his ankle and made himself so lame that the Government retired him from the Navy at twenty-eight years of age as physically unfit for service. Imagine yourself retired for physical incapacity before you were thirty. Some men would have thrown up their hands and admitted defeat.

But Dick Byrd didn't. He said a man didn't have to stand up to fly a plane; he could do that sitting down. He could do that even if he did have a lame foot and a broken ankle. So he started out to become an aviator and he succeeded, in spite of the fact that, while he was learning, he crashed twice and once he hit another plane head-on.

Thirsting for aerial adventure, he longed to fly over the frozen wastes of the North, where men had never flown before; but at every turn, he was refused and rebuffed. For example:

First, he planned to fly north in the huge dirigible, the *Shenandoah;* but the *Shenandoah* went up for a test flight and crashed. Then he pleaded with the Government to allow him to make test flights in order to fit a plane for crossing the Atlantic; but the Government wouldn't let him command the test flights because of his bad foot.

Next, he begged the Government to allow him to pilot

## ABOUT WELL KNOWN PEOPLE

one of the planes in which Amundsen planned to fly across the Arctic ice; and again he was refused, this time because he was married. And then, on top of all these bitter disappointments, he was retired from the navy a second time—retired again because he had a bad foot.

Of course, he may have been wrong, but Dick Byrd had the funny idea that initiative and courage and brains were more important than good feet. So he went out and got private parties to finance his expeditions, and then he set about doing things that startled the world. He flew across the Atlantic ocean. He dropped one American flag on the North Pole; and then he turned around and dropped another American flag on the South Pole; and when he returned to his native land, two million excited people gave him an ovation such as Rome never paid to Julius Caesar even when his chariots returned in triumph over Pompey's blood.

And finally, the United States Government conferred the title of Admiral on this young man who, fourteen years previously, it had retired.

*Drawing by Harry Furniss*
### REV. CHARLES L. DODGSON
He stammered when he talked to grown-ups

## HE WAS ASHAMED OF HAVING WRITTEN ONE OF THE MOST FAMOUS BOOKS IN THE WORLD

ONE day, about seventy years ago, a shy, timid, young man took three little girls out for a boat ride on the Thames River in England. When he stepped into the boat, this young man was unknown. But when he stepped out of it, three hours later, he was on his way to become one of the famous men of the nineteenth century.

His name was Dodgson. That is not the name you know him by; but that's his real name.

Sometimes he was called *Reverend* Dodgson and sometimes *Professor* Dodgson, for during the week, he taught mathematics in Oxford University, but on Sundays, he preached in a church.

When he tried to talk to grown-up people, he often became confused and stammered—but he always loved to tell nonsense stories to little girls. So, while out rowing his boat on the Thames River on this particular afternoon, he told a whimsical story to his three little companions.

He told them about a little girl who went to sleep and disappeared down a rabbit hole and awoke in Wonderland. They listened with wide-eyed astonishment, and forgot all about the boat ride and begged the professor to write the story for them; so he sat up all night doing it. And since one of the little girls had the name of Alice, he called the story *Alice in Wonderland*.

He put the story away, and forgot all about it, for it

never occurred to him that anyone would want to read it.

Years later, a friend of his came across the manuscript, brushed off the dust, read it, was enthralled by it and insisted on publishing it. But Professor Dodgson was shocked! What? Was he, a professor of mathematics in Oxford University, going to let the world know that he wrote a nonsense story for children? No! It was beneath his dignity! He wouldn't think of it.

So when *Alice in Wonderland* was published, it came out under an assumed name—the name of Lewis Carroll.

It was a tremendous success.

The book fairly enchanted the English-speaking world, was quickly translated into fourteen languages, and people everywhere, from Tennessee to Timbuctu, were soon repeating:

> *The time has come, the walrus said,*
> *To talk of many things.*
> *Of shoes, and ships, and sealing wax,*
> *And cabbages and kings.*
> *And why the sea is boiling hot,*
> *And whether pigs have wings.*

Year by year, *Alice in Wonderland* has grown in popularity. Printing presses, thundering day and night, have tossed off one hundred and sixty-nine editions in the English language alone. For seventy years, it has remained the most popular children's story in all the world.

## HE USES BAD ENGLISH BUT HE GETS FIVE DOLLARS A SECOND FOR TALKING

Who do you suppose makes more money than anyone else in the United States? I don't mean business men or people with investments. I mean the man who makes the largest income merely by the use of his own talents, without any business, without any investment, without having a lot of other people working for him.

Charlie Chaplin? No. Chaplin hasn't made a picture for two years; and besides, he is in business anyway, for he owns his own company.

Greta Garbo? No!

Amos 'n Andy? No!

Rudy Valee? No!

No, this biggest money-maker is a man who never had very much education. He uses bad English. He wears old clothes, he is lazy, he is always late to an appointment, and he loves to chew gum. His name is Will Rogers.

He gets $375,000 a year for making three pictures; and he gets $400 a day or $2,800 a week for his newspaper column. He gets a thousand dollars for merely making a funny speech. He gets $333 a minute for talking over the radio. Why, he can just pause between sentences and make ten or fifteen dollars.

He is fifty-four years old. He was born on Election Day and he has made half a million dollars cracking jokes about Congress, but he has never voted himself. Why?

WILLIAM PENN ADAIR ROGERS
He wanted to be a preacher

Because he was in the show business for twenty-four years and never lived in one place long enough to register and vote; and he doesn't like to vote now because he wants to be able to speak his mind without any party prejudice.

He was not born in one of the states of the United States. He was born in the Indian Territory. He was born in a ranch house, made of boards, four miles from a tiny, little place called Oologah. The house is still standing. A few years ago, the Chamber of Commerce put up a sign which said, "This way to see the house where Will Rogers was born." Naturally the tourists came in flocks and droves. They chipped and cut and carried off so many souvenirs that the sign had to be taken down and an iron chain locked around the gate leading to the ranch.

What do you suppose Will's mother wanted him to be? She wanted him to be a Methodist preacher! And during the first part of his life, Will himself planned to go into the ministry. His mother was a Methodist, and he is a Methodist right this minute. His mother was a great admirer of William Penn, so she named him William Penn Adair Rogers.

Both of his parents were part Indian—his mother one-fourth, and his father one-eighth. Will says he was never good at figures, and he can't figure out how much Indian that makes him. For years his father sat in the councils of the Cherokees as one of their wise men, and Will himself can talk some in the Cherokee language.

The first time Will ever came to New York he rode a freight train with a load of cattle. He fed and watered the cattle and slept sitting up in the caboose of the train all the way from Oklahoma to New York City. He walked up Broadway with his cowboy boots and his country clothes and of course people laughed at him. One man snatched off his hat and jeered at him. The last time he came by airplane, stopped at the Waldorf-Astoria, and when he walked along the street, people stopped and stared at him and crowded around him, begging for his autograph.

When he was a young man, Rogers wanted to see the world, so he went to South America, traveling steerage to save money. He got a job there punching cattle at four dollars a month.

When the Boer War broke out, he went to South Africa on a cattle boat and got a job breaking wild horses for the British cavalry.

When the war was over, he was so hard up that he had to live with the soldiers in the army barracks and eat handouts that the cook gave him. Wanting to get back to America, he joined a small traveling circus as a trick rider and rope-spinner under the name of "The Cherokee Kid." And that was the way Will Rogers broke into the show business.

He married Miss Betty Blake, a girl who was born in Arkansas. The first time he ever saw her, she was sitting on a front porch in Claremore, Oklahoma, drinking lemonade. He had just bought a new bicycle and wanted to show off; so he tried to do a bit of trick riding and fell off and hurt himself. Miss Blake rushed out and picked him up and helped wash a cut on his hand. That is the way he met Betty Blake. She is now Mrs. Will Rogers, and she has three children.

He lives practically all the time on a 260-acre ranch near Hollywood. He has a polo field on it, and his favorite way of entertaining his friends is to play polo with them.

## ABOUT WELL KNOWN PEOPLE

He has a nine-hole golf course on his ranch—but he never plays golf! He says he can't play any game unless it's got a horse or a rope in it."

There are many astonishing things about Will Rogers: he has met kings and queens and has been entertained by the high and the mighty of this earth—and yet he has never owned a long-tailed coat, and he has never worn a full dress suit except where he was compelled to, in a play or in a motion picture. His favorite food is *chili con carne*. He is insured for a million dollars. He seldom carries more than five dollars in his pocket. He has never had a chauffeur for himself. He used to be on the stage as a black-face comedian; at a party, he dearly loves to give imitations of Negroes; and one time over the radio he imitated Amos 'n Andy, Brother Crawford and the Kingfish. He does not smoke and he rarely chews gum when he is off the stage. And he never chews it around the house.

He wears old, dilapidated clothes and he frequently drives into Hollywood or Los Angeles without a necktie and wearing boots and old, blue denim overalls with brass rivets in them.

He is proud of his Indian ancestry. He says, "My folks didn't come over on the Mayflower, but when the Mayflower landed, we were there to meet them."

*Courtesy of New Outlook*
### DR. S. PARKES CADMAN
He reads two or three detective stories a week

## THE BEST KNOWN RADIO PREACHER IN THE WORLD HAS A "WICKED" BIBLE

From my home in New York, I occasionally cross the East River to spend a few delightful hours chatting with S. Parkes Cadman, of Brooklyn. Doctor Cadman is one of the best known men in America. You have probably heard him preach many times on the radio, for he has been broadcasting for eleven years. He was one of the pioneers in broadcasting. He thinks that Graham McNamee is the only other person still on the air who started when he did.

If you think you are busy, listen to what Doctor Cadman accomplishes in a day!

He gets up at seven o'clock, dictates twenty or thirty letters, writes fifteen hundred words for his newspaper column, prepares a sermon or works on a book he is writing, visits five or six of his parishioners, attends two or three meetings, makes a talk or two, dashes home, reads a new book completely through, then calls it a day and gets to sleep about two o'clock in the morning.

A program like that would make me dizzy in forty-eight hours but Doctor Cadman keeps it up month after month —and he is nearly seventy years old. Think of it! I once asked him how he did it. He said that was simple. He plans his work.

He declares that he saves one hour a day by dictating to a dictaphone instead of dictating to a secretary, and he told me that Gladstone taught him a valuable lesson about how to work. When Gladstone was managing the affairs of England for Queen Victoria, he had four desks in his office —one for literary work, one for correspondence, one for political affairs and one for his favorite studies. Gladstone found he could work better when he got variety; so he would work awhile at one desk and then move to another. Doctor Cadman does the same thing. He constantly varies his tasks, and he says that keeps him fresh and alert.

And he varies his reading too. If you imagine the learned Doctor Cadman is always pouring over pious books of theology, you are wrong. He believes that it is as necessary to have variety in your reading as in your eating. So he reads two or three detective stories every week. He loves "Sherlock Holmes" and he regards "The Hound of the Baskervilles" as the finest detective story ever written.

The day I called on him, I noticed four books on his desk. There was one explaining Doctor Hay's system of diet, one entitled "The Romance of Labrador" by Doctor Grenfell, there was the "Memoirs of the Court of Louis XIV," and a recently published murder story.

To me, one of the astonishing things about this astonishing man is the fact that he went to work in a coal mine in England when he was eleven years old, and for ten long years he continued to work underground for eight hours every day, to help support his younger brothers and sisters.

It didn't look then as if he was ever going to get an education. Yet today he is one of the most widely read men in America. He once told me that he had a fair knowledge of every branch of English literature. When he was working as a "pony boy," down in the coal mines, he always had to wait a minute or two each time his cart was unloaded; and while he waited, he dived into his pocket and pulled out a book. It was so dark down there in the mines that you couldn't see your hand before you; and he had to read by the light of a dim, dirty, old lantern; and he seldom had more than 120 seconds at a time in which he could read. Yet he always carried a book. He told me that he would rather have gone without lunch than to have gone without his books.

He knew there was only one way to get out of that coal mine, and that was to read himself out of it. So during the ten years that he worked as a coal miner, he read every book he could beg or borrow in the neighboring village —more than a thousand volumes. No wonder that boy got ahead. You couldn't have stopped him with anything less potent than a shot gun. Ten years after he started in the coal mine, he had educated himself sufficiently to pass his college examinations with honors and to win a scholarship at Richmond College, in London.

Doctor Cadman is now preaching every Sunday to more than five million people. He is one of the most famous preachers on earth. He is heard all over the world. Admiral Byrd once sent him a radiogram from Little America, telling him how much they were enjoying his talks down near the South Pole. Yet, when Dr. Cadman first came to America, he got a job preaching to only one hundred and fifty people in Millbrook, N. Y. They were supposed to pay him $600 a year, but they hadn't much money, so they used to give him pork and potatoes and apples and turkeys, instead of cash. One farmer gave him a load of hay.

Doctor Cadman was born in a little coal mining town called Old Park, in Shropshire, England; and Sally Partridge, one of the old neighbors, prophesied that he would grow up to be a thief because, when he was a baby, his mother cut his finger nails instead of biting them off.

Doctor Cadman told me that Abraham Lincoln had affected him more than any other man in all history. Thackeray is his favorite novelist, and his favorite poems are Wordsworth's "Ode to Immortality" and Milton's "Ode to the Nativity."

When I asked what his favorite food was, you should have seen the pained expression that came to his face. He said tragically, "Oh, my boy, I'm on a diet. I can eat hardly anything that I want to eat," and then he added, "Isn't it a pity that so many of the good things in life are forbidden—especially to us parsons."

Doctor Cadman collects etchings and antique furniture and he has a fine collection of rare books. He has one of the few copies in existence of the "wicked" Bible. It is called "wicked" because the "not" was left out of one of the Ten Commandments by mistake.

## HE WROTE 1200 VOLUMES AND BOASTED THAT HE HAD 500 CHILDREN

What is the most popular adventure story ever written? *Robinson Crusoe? Don Quixote? Treasure Island?* Naturally, opinions differ; but I'll cast my vote for *The Three Musketeers*.

*The Three Musketeers* has been a "best seller" for almost a century. Your grandmother probably thrilled to it in the theater when she was a girl, and hundreds of people are reading it this very minute, in a dozen different languages, all over the world.

Alexander Dumas, the man who wrote *The Three Musketeers*, was one of the most astonishing novelists that ever dipped a goose quill into ink. He loved to boast that he had more than five hundred children. His estimate may have been a trifle optimistic; but in spite of his fat, grotesque appearance, he did have a way with women. He declared over and over again that he would never marry. But he boasted once too often and one of his sweethearts called his bluff. She had her guardian buy up all of Alexander's debts at a bargain price. In those days, you could be clamped into jail for debt; so Dumas, the great lover, was politely informed that he could take his choice—marry or go to the hoosegow. He married.

Dumas even *looked* strange. Three-fourths of the blood that coursed through his arteries was white; but the other fourth was negro. His grandmother had been a negro slave

ALEXANDER DUMAS
He fought twenty duels with swords and pistols

on a sugar plantation in the West Indies. Her name had been Marie Dumas. Poor and uneducated, she lived and died in complete obscurity, never dreaming that her grandson would be honored by princes and poets and plutocrats, and make her name famous throughout the world.

Alexander Dumas looked a lot like his negro grandmother. To be sure, his skin was snowy white, and his eyes were as blue as the West Indian sky. But his lips were thick, his nostrils wide and flat; and his hair, though yellow as a buttercup, was just as kinky and frizzy as his old negro grandmother's.

An epicure and a gourmet, he was nearly as famous for his ability to concoct a sauce or roast a duck as for his ability to write a novel. He would consume a meal of caviar, *pate de foie gras,* fish, filet mignon, roast partridge, half a dozen kind of vegetables, and top it off with vast quantities of cheese. He would eat a meal that would have put even Bismarck to shame; yet, in spite of his gluttonous appetite, he never drank liquor or coffee, and he never smoked. When he was busy writing, he didn't even care about food; and sometimes he even forgot to eat at all. If a friend dropped in to see him while he was working, he simply held out his left hand in greeting and kept on scribbling with his right hand.

But he was frightfully temperamental about the kind of paper and pens he used.

For example, he could only write novels on blue paper, and with a special set of pens. If he was writing poetry, he used yellow paper and a different set of pens. If he was writing an article for a magazine, he couldn't possibly use anything but rose-colored writing paper; and he never, under any circumstances, used blue ink. Blue ink gave him the jitters. And he couldn't compose a play while sitting at his desk. In order to write a play, he had to lie down on a sofa with a good soft pillow propped under his elbow.

Ridiculous? Yes, but before you laugh at him, let me tell you what he accomplished. He wrote over one hundred plays and so many novels and histories that the collected edition of his entire work today totals one thousand, two hundred volumes! Think of it! One thousand, two hundred volumes! That is almost twice the entire output of John Galsworthy, George Bernard Shaw, Robert Louis Stevenson, H. G. Wells, Rudyard Kipling, Mary Roberts Rinehart and Zane Grey taken all together.

He earned over five million dollars—far, far more than any other writer of his age. In fact, very few writers in all history have ever approached such a record. Yet he was so poor when his first play opened that he didn't have a collar to wear to the theater. He actually cut a collar out of a piece of white carboard, and wore that to one of the biggest events of his life.

This fat, flashily dressed giant adored his mother. And just three days before his first play opened, his mother became paralyzed. So, on the night of his first great triumph, in Paris, Alexander left the theater at the end of each act, and ran, as fast as his long legs could carry him, to his mother's bedside, to see if she needed anything. And that night, with the whole of Paris ringing with his name, he slept on a mattress at the foot of his mother's bed.

The characters in Dumas' books were intensely real to him. He dreamed about them and gossiped about them just as if they were living people; and he wrote about them with a sweep and gusto that holds you spell-bound

## ABOUT WELL KNOWN PEOPLE

now, almost a hundred years later. Sometimes he would be carried away completely with his story and he would shout with laughter and joke with his characters as if they were actually sitting across the table from him. Most novelists find writing to be a terrible grind. But Dumas had a gorgeous time spinning his rollicking tales.

Blessed with the energy of a Jack Dempsey, he tore all over Europe by stage coach and horseback, and he often kept five novels going all at one time, appearing, day by day, as serials in the newspapers. He didn't have time to read his own books; but he did have time to fight twenty duels with swords and pistols.

As he grew older, he went in for wine, women and song. No. No. I am wrong. He didn't drink and he didn't sing; but he did go in for girls in a big way.

If Paris is anything, it is broad-minded. Yet Dumas' love life became a sensation and a scandal even in gay Paree. Finally his own son turned from him in disgust.

Once, a friend called on the great novelist, in the middle of the afternoon, and found him almost smothered with girls. One was sitting on his knee, another was lying at his feet, and still another was standing behind his chair and leaning over to kiss his puffy lips; and all three of these girls didn't have on enough clothes to make a respectable bathing suit for a humming bird.

When the many gold diggers had extracted all his money, they deserted him, in derision and contempt, and Dumas spent his old age in poverty and loneliness and neglect. He had to pawn his jewelry and even his overcoat to pay the rent, and he would have gone hungry if his son hadn't paid the grocery bills.

Shortly before he died, his son found him reading a

copy of *The Three Musketeers*. "How do you like it, father?" he asked, and the old man said "It'll do. It's good."

Good? I'll say it's good. And if you want to give yourself a treat, pick up *The Three Musketeers* and read it over again. Millions of other novels have been written since it appeared, and have faded away into the limbo of oblivion. *The Three Musketeers* is immortal; and a couple of hundred years from now your great, great, great, great, great grandchildren will be sitting up nights to read it.

## A CYCLONE IN PETTICOATS WHO STARTLED AMERICA

On January 21, 1901, one of the most sensational women in American history walked down the streets of Wichita, Kansas, singing "Onward Christian Soldiers." She had a hatchet in her hand and when she reached Jim Burn's saloon on Douglas Avenue, she rushed in through the swinging doors, waved her hatchet in the air and shouted: "This is the arm of God. I have come to save you men from a drunkard's hell."

The customers fled out of the side door.

The bartender ducked behind a table, while Carry Nation threw beer bottles at the mirrors and smashed in the heads of whisky barrels with her hatchet. In a few minutes, the place looked as if it had been struck by a Kansas cyclone.

And it had. It had been struck by a cyclone in petticoats.

Carry Nation, the Joan of Arc of prohibition, was on the war path and telegraph wires and cables flashed the news all over the world.

By her fiery and spectacular crusades, she helped arouse the indignation that made national prohibition possible seventeen years later.

Carry Nation had good and sufficient reasons for despising the saloon. Whisky had broken up her home. Her husband had died a drunkard's death, leaving her penniless, with a baby to support. She had tried at first to close the

**CARRY NATION**
She was knocked down, kicked, horse-whipped, beaten with clubs
until her bones were broken

saloons in Kansas by preaching and prayer. She would often set up an old organ on the sidewalk, in front of a saloon, and sing and pray for the saloon keeper's soul. She actually closed several saloons in that way. But that method was too slow for Carry Nation. She wanted action. So she started throwing brickbats and smashing saloons with her hatchet. Of course, she knew she was breaking the law, but she also knew the saloons were breaking the law, for Kansas had been dry for twenty years.

Was she afraid? Never! She was knocked down and kicked and horse-whipped and beaten with clubs until her bones were broken and she was almost dead. But nothing could stop her, for she believed she was acting on orders direct from the Almighty. She believed God came and spoke to her in visions. Sometimes, when she opened her Bible, she heard the flutter of angel's wings. Sometimes, she found every word in her Bible glowing with a soft, luminous light.

It didn't do any good to throw her into jail for she immediately began to sing and praise God. She kept many a Kansas jail humming with her songs.

When she was dragged into court, she insisted on acting as her own attorney and when the judge quoted the laws of Kansas she cried: "We are not going to try this case according to the laws of Kansas. We are going to try it according to the laws of Ecclesiastes." And then she would stand up and begin reading her Bible.

When the judge told her to sit down, she snapped back at him, "Don't you tell me to sit down. I'm old enough to be your mother."

After her first husband died, Carry Nation taught school to support herself, her baby and her mother-in-law. At the end of four years, she lost her position and then got down on her knees and prayed thus: "My Lord, I can't take care of mother and Charlien, and I want you to help me. If it be best for me to marry, I will do so. I have no one picked out, dear Lord, but I want you to select the one that you think best. . . ."

A few months later, she married David Nation, a newspaper editor, farmer and preacher. She thought their marriage was an answer to prayer. David Nation finally became pastor of a church in Holton, Kansas. But Carry felt she knew more about preaching than her husband did; so she chose his texts for him and often wrote his sermons. While David stood in the pulpit trying to inspire his little flock, Carry sat in the front row and told him in audible tones when to raise and lower his voice, when to speed it up and where to gesture. When she thought he had preached long enough, she would step out into the aisle and say in a loud voice: "That will be all for today, David." If he didn't stop preaching immediately, she marched right up to the pulpit, banged the Bible shut under his nose, handed him his hat and told him to go home.

After a few months of this, the Church Board asked their pastor to resign and he did so with pleasure.

Years later, when he sued her for a divorce, she said, "David was too slow for me."

That girl didn't need a husband; she needed a Kansas jack rabbit.

I feel especially at home on the subject of Carry Nation. Although she was born about half a century before I was, I lived in the same town where she and part of the Jesse James gang had grown up. For awhile, I attended the same college that she had attended; and she is buried now in my

## ABOUT WELL KNOWN PEOPLE

home town of Belton, Missouri. I expect to be buried there myself, so I will probably lie within a few yards of Carry Nation throughout countless centuries of time.

I once saw her in action in a church, in Pierre, South Dakota. The preacher said something that morning that she didn't like; and she spoke right up in church, then and there, and told him what she thought.

On another occasion, I saw her walk up to a man in a crowd, knock a cigar out of his mouth and tell him that he ought to be ashamed of himself, for tobacco made him smell like a dog. She was opposed to almost everything except horse racing. She had been born down in Kentucky, so of course she thought horse racing was all right. But I have seen her stop young women on the street and warn them not to go buggy riding with young men.

When she came to New York, she caused an uproar by going to the swanky horse show in Madison Square Garden and publicly denouncing Mrs. Alfred Vanderbilt for wearing evening clothes.

Was Carry Nation crazy? Well, her daughter had to be shut up in an insane asylum; and Carry may not have been entirely sane herself. But who is?

She did many beautiful things. For example, her father died, leaving a lot of debts; and fifteen years later, she paid those debts. She didn't have to, and no one expected her to, but she did.

In the last few years of her life, she made considerable money by lecturing; but she gave it away to the poor and hungry; and she built a home in Kansas City for the wives and orphans of drunkards.

When Carry Nation first began breathing fire on the plains of Kansas, the anti-saloon movement was a weak, impotent affair. But Carry Nation transformed it into a militant giant that eventually put the 18th amendment into the Constitution.

The State of Kansas has named one of its highways in her honor. It is called "The Carry Nation Trail," and the signs on it are hatchets.

# THE RICHEST MAN IN THE WORLD EATS
## SOUP WITH HIS FINGERS

THE richest man in the world eats with his fingers. He doesn't use a knife, nor a fork, nor a spoon. He even drinks his soup out of his fingers.

I am not referring to the fastidious Mr. Morgan, nor to the temperate Mr. Rockefeller, nor to the bustling Mr. Ford.

No, the richest man in the world has never played the stock market. He has never seen Wall Street; and most of the people in America have never even heard of him.

His name is Nizam Osman Ali Khan Bahadur Fateh Jung Asaf Jah; but he is usually called the Nizam of Hyderabad, and he is a descendant of the old Mogul Emperors who swept down through the Kyber Pass and looted India centuries ago. He rules with a high hand over the richest state in India.

What does he do with all his wealth? Well, for one thing, he has a harem filled with over five hundred women.

But he has one favorite, and she rides around in a Rolls-Royce limousine, with the shades drawn, so that the unworthy populace cannot gaze upon her royal face. He doesn't pay much attention to the other beauties in his harem. Did I say "beauties?" Well, now that is a bit of exaggeration, for he inherited his harem from his father who died twenty-three years ago. These Harem girls may have been regular Jean Harlows twenty-three years ago;

NIZAM OF HYDERABAD
He could buy and sell Rockefeller and Morgan, but he sleeps
in a bed with no springs

but none of them could make the grade in an Atlantic City Beauty Contest now, for the passing of the years has left the tell-tale marks upon them. However, the Nizam is so strict with them that he will not even permit eunuchs in his harem.

The richest man in the world gets up every morning before dawn. But he doesn't have to jump out of bed and turn off the alarm clock, for His Exalted Highness is awakened from his dreams by a group of musicians who come into his presence playing and singing. Being a Mohammedan, he gets up early so that he can spread out his prayer rug, turn his face toward Mecca, prostrate himself before Allah, and pour out his soul in prayer as the sun looms over the hills of Hyderabad.

He has four servants whose sole duty in life is to dress him. Each servant dresses a different part of the royal body. One man, for example, is the trouser specialist. He would be insulted if you asked him to help put on the royal shirt. No sir, when he gets on the Nizam's trousers, he sits in the shade and rests up for the next morning's work.

The Nizam is an absolute monarch, with the power of life and death over fifteen million of his subjects; and the common people fling themselves humbly upon the ground as he passes by.

Although he takes a perfumed bath every morning, he doesn't use soap. He uses the powdered bark of a tree instead. He doesn't have breakfast until four hours after he gets up; and then he has a sort of combination breakfast and lunch. He doesn't drink tea or coffee—just milk or plain cold water.

He eats breakfast on plates of gold. And what a breakfast. A dozen different kinds of hot soups; eggs boiled and curried and scrambled and stuffed and fried. His jaded palate is tempted by such rare dishes as curried peacocks and wild cranes and bird of paradise.

He usually wears a white, silk coat, embroidered with gold, and has strings of pearls and diamonds looped about his neck; yet he has been seen in public, clad in a black tunic spotted with grease.

Although he has a barber, whose only duty in life is to keep him well groomed, he slips occasionally and goes about with his hair uncombed and his chin unshaved.

The Nizam of Hyderabad has chairs, couches, carriages, and even cannon, cast in solid gold and inlaid with emeralds and rubies. Of course, he can't shoot these golden cannon, because they are too soft, but they do make a mighty impression upon the visitor.

Where did the Nizam get all this wealth? A lot of it came from the valley of Golconda, the richest diamond field in the world. From the incredibly rich Golconda mines have come the most celebrated jewels in the world—jewels such as the huge, gleaming Kohinoor, now worn by Princess Mary of England; the ill-fated Hope diamond, that has left a trail of superstition and blood in its wake; the enormous Orloff diamond, which Catherine the Great bore aloft on her despotic sceptre.

And in spite of all his incredible wealth, the Nizam likes to make a few dollars on the side, even as you and I. For example, he gives sumptuous banquets, and his invited guests are expected to bring a suitable present in cash. He sometimes has five hundred guests for dinner—and, at ten dollars a head, you can figure it out for yourself.

He goes on regular shopping expeditions into the public market, tasting this food and that, and whenever His

## ABOUT WELL KNOWN PEOPLE

Exalted Highness admires anything, custom demands that the shopkeeper give it to him free of charge. So he goes back to the palace with an army of servants carrying baskets of food that didn't cost him a cent; and he sometimes sends these baskets to his friends with a price tag on each basket, specifying the amount that the friend must pay for the honor of receiving the gift.

About twelve years ago, the Nizam announced that he was going to publish a book of his own poems. The ordinary copies were going to cost twenty dollars, and the royal copies were going to cost a hundred. Since none of the aristocracy of Hyderabad dared refuse to buy the songs of the Imperial Poet, the book sold like hot cakes in advance of publication. Years have passed since then, but the royal poems have never been printed, and the money has never been returned.

The Nizam speaks perfect English, shoots tigers from the back of an elephant, wears rings in his ears, gives his favorite wife two hundred dollars a month for spending money, and sleeps in a bed that doesn't have any springs.

LENIN
Cakes, flower-beds and rugs bear these features

## ONCE HE SLEPT IN A PACKING BOX—
## TODAY HE IS WORSHIPPED AS A GOD

I WANT to tell you some little known facts about a man who has been dead only ten years; and yet a city of seven hundred thousand people has been named in his honor; and a hundred million people regard him as their Patron Saint.

His name was Lenin, and he started in Russia the greatest economic experiment the world has ever known—an experiment that is bound to have some effect on you and me and almost everyone else in the world.

Lenin was a little, bald-headed, wrinkled man; and when he sat in a chair, his legs were so short that they hardly touched the floor.

He didn't care anything at all about his looks; his trousers were usually too long, his nose was slightly turned up, he had a squint in one eye and he probably never wore a silk hat or a frock coat in his life. He was happily married, and his wife loved him so much that she refused to leave him when he was exiled; so she went with him into exile in order to look after him and care for him.

He had a lot of spare time when he was an outcast in Siberia, so he became an expert chess player. He could play several games of chess at the same time; and he was so fascinated with chess that he used to play the game with his friends far away by mail.

As a child, Lenin was serious and gloomy, seldom played

with other children and never took part in athletic games. When he grew to be a man, he had no interest whatever in music or poetry or religion; but he studied law and spoke four languages—French, German, Russian, and English.

The Russian government hanged his brother because he was plotting to kill Czar Alexander the Third; and the Government later banished Lenin himself because of his radical opinions. They banished him to a small town in frigid Siberia. There Lenin saw, with his own eyes, the tragic poverty of the Russian peasants. They were so poor they could not afford to eat meat except on the great religious holidays—in other words, they ate meat about twenty times a year.

During the great famine of 1891, when millions of poverty-stricken peasants died of starvation, and typhus and cholera, Lenin became convinced that something radical had to be done. From that time on, he became a flaming revolutionist.

During the next twenty-five years, he was hounded and driven from one country to another, living at various times in Germany, Austria, France, Poland, Switzerland and England. When he lived in London, he would often go and sit for hours at a time beside the grave of Karl Marx, the father of Socialism.

Sometimes, in order to escape arrest, he went about disguised as a peasant, or sailor, or factory worker. Sometimes he wore false whiskers. Sometimes he masqueraded as a woman. He always traveled with a false bottom in his trunk—and beneath the false bottom, he kept secret papers and incriminating documents. Sometimes he buried his

# ABOUT WELL KNOWN PEOPLE

secret documents in his vegetable garden and he planted onions and cabbage above them.

He wrote one of his revolutionary books in prison; and, in order to avoid detection, he wrote it in milk instead of ink. The writing could be read only after it was dipped in hot water. He taught his disciples to use invisible ink when they wrote to him. When he got one of these invisible letters, he would ask the prison guard for tea. Then, as soon as the guard's back was turned, he would dip the letter in the hot water and read the letter.

In November, 1917, Lenin became dictator of Russia and confiscated all private property. The owners of the great estates fled in terror, as the peasants took possession. The peasants cut up rare and exquisite tapestries and made them into shoes. They took priceless vases, made by the master potters of Europe, and used them for pickle jars.

Russia was almost starving at the time and Lenin refused to take sugar in his tea because other people couldn't have sugar. Although he was the supreme ruler of Russia, he wouldn't permit himself to have even the simplest luxuries. He ruled Russia without having a staff of secretaries and he rarely dictated a letter. He worked from eighteen to twenty hours a days and wrote almost all his letters himself.

Five years later, he was suffering from hardening of the arteries, and he had a stroke of paralysis. He lost the power of speech, and he had to learn to talk all over again like a child. His right hand was paralyzed so he learned to write with his left hand. For two years, he fought desperately with death, saying over and over again, "There is so much work left for me to do."

His picture hangs today in almost every house, every factory and every worker's club in all Russia. The bakers put his likeness on the top of their cakes. Gardeners plant their flowers so that they will blossom into his portrait and the carpet makers weave his features into their rugs. Millions of people worship him almost as if he were a God and the peasants are already telling miracle stories of his return from the grave to help some worker who is in trouble.

His body now lies embalmed in a glass casket; and probably at this very moment, hundreds of reverent pilgrims are filing by it with uncovered heads. Nearly a thousand a day do him this honor. And at this very instant, Red soldiers, with bayonets, are standing guard over the man who ushered in a new era in the history of the world.

## HE MADE THOUSANDS OF MILLIONAIRES AND DIED WITH HOLES IN HIS SHOES

Two hundred years ago, a foreigner in France, a Scotsman called "Handsome John" Law, came to Paris—friendless and unknown, and made himself financial dictator of France and the most powerful man in Europe. Twelve years later, he fled in disgrace with an infuriated mob howling for his blood and longing to tear him limb from limb.

The doings of this handsome Scotsman—half Casanova and half John Stuart Mill—constitute one of the most bizarre and spectacular tales in all the annals of adventure. His wild cat schemes made beggars of half a nation and his fantastic Mississippi Bubble has gone down into history as a byword for financial folly.

At the age of twelve, John Law was a precocious and brilliant mathematician who astonished the professors of Edinburgh. At seventeen, he was a dandy and a fop, pinching snuff with a graceful flourish and strutting about in a curled wig and a rose-colored silk coat, ruffled with lace.

At twenty, he was a notorious gambler, addicted to the shuffle of cards and the rattle of dice. At twenty-six, he fell in love with an old man's darling; and the old man, consumed with jealous rage, challenged the young Scotsman to a duel. They fought in a thick London fog and John Law killed his adversary with a sword.

Law was arrested, tried for murder, and sentenced to be

## JOHN LAW
He told them Louisiana was an Eldorado, rich with gold and sparkling with emeralds

hanged by the neck till dead. But two days before he was to mount the gallows, he drugged his guards, slipped out of his chains, scaled the prison walls, and escaped to France.

These were terrible times. French mobs, driven to desperation by hate and hunger, boiled through the streets of Paris, smashing statues of their dead king, Louis the Fourteenth, and demanding that the new government do something at once to save the country from starvation and disaster.

And presto! John Law appeared with his glib tongue and his radical ideas. He persuaded the Government to print a little paper money. Prices rose. Business hummed. Happy days were there again and "Handsome John" Law was regarded as a miracle man. So he started doing a bit of promoting. He organized a great monopoly, an industrial octopus which had the exclusive rights to trade with China, India, the South Seas, Canada, and all the French colonies in America.

John Law ballyhooed his new project in glamorous terms. Louisiana was a modern Eldorado, rich with gold and sparkling with emeralds. With a lordly touch of magnificence, John Law guaranteed to pay dividends of one hundred and twenty per cent a year on his project. Prices leaped and skyrocketed, and the public went mad.

Dukes and dishwashers, counts and cut-throats, all fought with one another in a desperate effort to get inside Law's house and buy more stock. The jam was so terrible, the impact so terrific, that people were crushed to death in the hysterical mob.

The Government kept the printing presses busy turning out more money, and John Law kept issuing more stock. The boom swept over France like a tornado. Everybody was getting rich. Servants and stable boys speculated in the stocks and woke up in the morning to find themselves millionaires.

A Duchess, going to the Opera, was astounded to discover that the box next to hers was occupied by her former cook, now bedecked with glittering diamonds.

The streets of Paris resembled a Mardi Gras. Side shows and refreshment booths crowded the highways; roulette wheels whirled and clicked, and pickpockets from the gutters of Europe fattened on the infatuated mobs.

The population of Paris increased by three hundred thousand. Inns and lodgings were stuffed like barracks. Thrifty housewifes earned tidy fortunes making up beds in their attics and kitchens—even in their stables. The streets were so jammed with vehicles that a foot-pace was the speed limit. Prices soared and wages went rocketing after them. Factories hummed night and day—villas were being built everywhere, and all la belle France was riding towards Bagdad in a gilded coach.

Then came the first, faint rumble of impending disaster. The powerful Prince of Conti, in a moment of anger, filled three wagons with paper money, and driving to the bank, spitefully demanded gold. Another man put his fortune into a farmer's cart, covered it with hay, and then, disguised as a peasant, in wooden shoes, drove his load of francs and fodder over the border into Belgium.

The Mississippi Bubble burst. Confidence was gone—gone as quickly and dramatically as it had come. The bank stopped payment. John Law was dismissed in disgrace and France was gripped by a panic. The crowd that had once elbowed and gouged one another in a frantic scramble

# ABOUT WELL KNOWN PEOPLE

to buy stock, now trampled fourteen people to death in a mad effort to get its money back.

The infuriated mob hurled stones through the windows of Law's house and threatened to batter the life out of him.

Law, trembling in terror, fled from France leaving all his treasures behind. His gorgeous estates, worth millions of dollars, were confiscated. His books and furniture and silverware were sold. His wife and daughters became paupers. And nine years later, "Handsome John" Law, the man who had once been mightier and richer than kings, died in Venice, without friends and without money. There were holes in the bottom of his worn shoes, and he was too poor to buy a little bundle of wood to heat the miserable room in which he lay dying.

Lowell Thomas
RECEIVED
266,000 TELEGRAMS
IN RESPONSE TO A SINGLE BROADCAST

## HE GOT A QUARTER OF A MILLION TELE-
## GRAMS IN LESS THAN AN HOUR

THE Western Union Telegraph Company recently announced over the radio that, for one evening, it would send telegrams to Lowell Thomas free. Instantly, the wires all over America began to hum and "Tommy" was deluged with an avalanche of more than a quarter of a million messages in less than sixty minutes.

Lowell Thomas is one of the most extraordinary men I have ever known. He has written so many books he can hardly remember the names of all of them himself; and he has spoken to four million people, face to face, in more than four thousand audiences in every English-speaking country on the globe.

Week after week, month after month, I saw people in London stand in line for hours—stand in lines that were literally blocks long—to buy tickets to hear Lowell Thomas tell the fascinating story of Allenby's campaign in Palestine and Lawrence's exploits in Arabia.

He has been a gold miner, a cow puncher, a newspaper reporter and editor, and a college professor; and he has spent years roaming around Europe, Asia, Africa, Alaska, Australia, and the islands of the Seven Seas. He toured India with the Prince of Wales and was one of the first Americans ever to be given permission to enter the wild country of Afghanistan.

He and his camera men photographed the fighting armies

of Great Britain, France, Belgium, Italy, Serbia, America, and Arabia; and the Government of India gave him special trains and river steamers and placed strings of elephants at his command so that he could photograph the strange sights and the strange peoples of Mother India.

He formerly taught Public Speaking at Princeton University; and he is now probably the best known speaker living. He not only broadcasts the day's news to millions of listeners in America, but his voice encircles the globe. Sheep herders hear him down under in Australia and criminals listen to him at Sing Sing. His "fan" mail includes letters from diamond miners in South Africa and sea captains in Singapore.

Huge crowds flock to hear Mr. Thomas wherever he speaks. For instance, I saw a news item recently telling how, in Altoona, Pennsylvania, seven thousand people clamored to get within the sound of his voice. And in the past fifteen years that has been happening from Boston to Edinburgh, from San Francisco to Melbourne.

And how old do you suppose he is? With a record like that, he ought to have a beard as white as Bernard Shaw's; but he is only a little past forty, and he hasn't a grey hair in his head.

I first met Lowell Thomas nineteen years ago, when he was a student at Princeton University, working for a PH.D. degree in Constitutional Law. He had no money then, and no fame. How has success affected him? Has it changed him? Most assuredly no. He is the same kind, modest, unselfish and unassuming "Tommy" today that he was then.

He has an apartment at the swanky Waldorf-Astoria, in New York; but he would infinitely rather spend his time on his three-hundred-acre farm up in the Berkshire Hills, in Dutchess County, seventy miles North of New York City.

Getting back to the farm every night is almost a passion with him. He finishes his broadcast in Radio City at seven o'clock sharp. The last train for his home leaves the Grand Central Station five minutes later. Dash as fast as he can, through the city's traffic, he can't quite make it. So the New York Central Railroad has issued an order that the seven-five train must not pull out until Lowell Thomas is aboard. A round trip of one hundred and forty miles a day is the price he pays to spend the night and the next forenoon at "Clover Brook Farm."

When he was ten years old, "Tommy" was selling newspapers in the gambling halls and saloons of Cripple Creek, Colorado, one of the toughest gold mining camps that ever reverberated to the crack of pistol fire; yet "Tommy" himself doesn't smoke, he doesn't drink, he doesn't gamble. The truth is, he lives as quietly as a poet. His one abiding interest in life is his home and his family. He is married to a Colorado girl and he has a boy, "Sonny," eleven years old.

He is paid five hundred dollars a night for speaking in public; yet he doesn't talk much in private. He prefers to listen to other people talk.

I have often seen him, on a winter evening, stretch out on the floor in front of the fireplace with his dogs, and lie there for hours, staring into the flames, without saying a word.

"Tommy" had very little cash when he started out to get an education; so he worked his way through four universities by caring for furnaces, acting as a cook and waiter, feeding a cow for a professor, selling real estate, and doing a bit of teaching on the side.

And he has a herd of cows now—but if "Tommy" ever milked one himself, it has escaped my notice. If you ever visit his farm, don't look for him in the cow barn. You are much more likely to find him diving in the swimming pool, monkeying around his mink and fitch and fox pens, fooling with "Nudist" his black bear, or riding a horse.

The New York Police Department once found itself in possession of a couple of snorty mustangs—horses so wild and jumpy that it was dangerous to use them in city traffic. One of them ran away, dashed down Fifth Avenue, smashed up a parade and bucked a cop onto the sidewalk. So the police offered these wild-eyed cayuses to "L. T." and he rode 'em over the Berkshire Hills until their bodies were white with foamy lather and their spirits were subdued.

He is one of the busiest men I have ever known, and yet he never seems to be in a hurry. He is always calm and relaxed. For example, I remember one winter day when I was at his farm and we had to catch an early train to New York. We figured we had just seven minutes in which to eat breakfast, and the rest of us were in a nervous hurry; but "Tommy" calmly strolled into the dining room and wanted to build a fire in the fireplace so he could look at it while he was eating.

Lowell Thomas is perhaps the only man in the world who learned to fly an airplane before he learned to drive an automobile.

## COLUMBUS WAS THE THIRD MAN TO DISCOVER AMERICA

ON every 12th of October, we celebrate one of the most important events in our history, the discovery of America by Christopher Columbus; but here is a funny thing— Columbus did not discover America on October 12th. He discovered it on October 23rd. The calendar we are using now was originated by Pope Gregory. Columbus never heard of that calendar: it didn't even exist until one hundred years after he was dead. The American colonies adopted that calendar in 1752; and when we adopted it, we jumped time ahead exactly 11 days. Why? Because the calendar at that time was eleven days behind the sun. So, according to the present calendar, Columbus discovered America, not on October 12th, but on October 23rd.

As a young man, Columbus had gone to sea on a pirate ship. There wasn't anything strange about that, for in those days, the best families sent their boys out on pirate ships. It gave the lads self-confidence and salt air; enabled them to see the world, and make a little money on the side; and there was not the slightest disgrace about it unless you were caught—and then it was just too bad.

As a boy in school, Columbus had studied a book by Pythagoras, who taught that the world was round. So Columbus got an idea. He figured out that, if it was round, he could find a short cut to India; and that would make him a fortune.

CHRISTOPHER COLUMBUS

His sailors were terror-stricken and wanted to turn back

## ABOUT WELL KNOWN PEOPLE

But the learned professors and philosophers in the universities laughed at his silly idea. What? Did this crazy fool propose to reach India which was out in the east by sailing directly west? Why, the man must be a lunatic. They told him that the earth was not round, but flat; and they warned him that he would be committing suicide; that his ships would sail to the edge of the world and then tumble off into unending space.

For seventeen years, Columbus tried to get someone to finance his adventure. He tried for seventeen years, and he failed for seventeen years. Finally, he was ready to give up in despair; and he retired to a monastery in Spain to end his days. He wasn't quite fifty years old then, but he had had so much trouble and so much heartbreak that his red hair had become snow white.

Finally, the Pope in Rome urged Queen Isabella of Spain to help Columbus. So the Queen sent him sixty-five dollars and Columbus, being in rags, bought a new suit of clothes and a donkey and set out to see the Queen. He was so poor, he had to beg for his food on the way.

The Queen gave him the ships that he needed, but he found it almost impossible to get a crew. Everyone was afraid to go. So he went down to the waterfront and boldly seized some sailors and forced them to go. He begged and bribed and threatened others. He even took criminals out of jails, and offered them their freedom if they would go.

Finally, everything was in readiness; and one-half hour before sunrise, on Friday, August 3, 1492, Columbus with his three ships and eighty-eight men, set out on one of the most important and epoch-making journeys in the history of the world.

The colonies that Columbus founded in the new world met with nothing but disappointment and disaster. All the people in the first colony were murdered by the Indians. The Governor of the second colony was so jealous of Columbus that he accused him of all sorts of crimes, had him arrested and sent back to Spain in chains. To be sure, he was turned loose as soon as he reached Spain, but the chagrin and disappointment of it all broke his heart.

Columbus died at the age of sixty—unnoticed, unhonored and unsung. He died in a shabby, poorly-ventilated room, and on the walls of the room hung the chains that he had worn as a prisoner. He kept them hanging there as a grim reminder of the vanity of this world and its ingratitude.

Columbus had accomplished one of the most amazing and courageous feats in history. And yet what did he get out of it? He had expected to make a fortune, and he died a pauper. He had been promised the title of "Admiral of the Ocean and Viceroy of India." Yet he got no title whatever. The continent that he discovered was not even named for him. It was named for a maker of maps, Amerigo Vespucci. In fact, about the only thing that he ever got out of discovering a new world was heartbreak and disgrace.

He didn't even get the satisfaction of realizing that he had reached a new continent. He thought he had merely found a new way to India, and that is why he gave the name of Indians to the red-skinned people that he found in America.

However, Columbus has gotten one "break." He is given credit for being the first man to discover America, when he wasn't at all. A thousand years before Columbus

# ABOUT WELL KNOWN PEOPLE

was born, Hoe-Shin, a Buddhist monk from China, discovered America; and then, 500 years before Columbus was born, a Norseman by the name of Lief Ericson, discovered it again, and you can still see what historians believe are the ruins of the houses that Lief Ericson built on the banks of the Charles River in Massachusetts. In fact, they are within walking distance of Harvard University.

Columbus will be forever honored in history as a man of heroic courage and unflinching determination. When everybody else wanted to quit, he kept on. When his sailors became terror-stricken and threatened to mutiny and kill him, unless he turned back, Columbus had only one answer for them. "Sail on! Sail on! And on!"

> *Behind him lay the gray Azores,*
> *Behind the Gates of Hercules;*
> *Before him not the ghost of shores;*
> *Before him only shoreless seas.*
> *The good mate said: "Now must we pray,*
> *For lo! the very stars are gone.*
> *Brave Ad'r'l, speak; what shall I say?"*
> *"Why, say: 'Sail on! sail on! and on!'"*

**CARRIE JACOBS BOND**
She ran a rooming house, painted china, wrote her songs on wrapping paper

## SHE SANG IN OLD LACE CURTAINS AND WROTE THE MOST POPULAR SONG OF THE 20TH CENTURY

ONE white frozen night, about forty years ago, far up among the dense pine forests of Northern Michigan, Doctor Frank Bond, a physician, left home to call on a patient. As he was leaving, he kissed his wife goodbye and said, "My darling, it gets harder every day to say goodbye to you. But that is the way it should be, for love is the greatest thing in the world. We know, because we're still lovers."

Those were almost the last words he ever spoke, for five minutes later Doctor Bond was hurled to the ground and lay writhing under the pains of oncoming death. A child, shouting, and throwing snowballs, had rushed up behind Dr. Bond and given him a playful shove. Slipping on the treacherous ice, he fell on the frozen ground, crushing his ribs, and died in terrible agony.

Four thousand dollars in life insurance, a load of debts, and a little boy to support—such was the legacy the good doctor bequeathed to his bewildered widow, Carrie Jacobs Bond.

She had had no business experience whatever. She didn't know how to do anything except keep house; and she could hardly do even that, for she had been an invalid for years, her body racked and tortured by the terrible pangs of inflammatory rheumatism.

But she didn't want pity and she didn't want charity. She was too proud for that. So she cut herself off from all her friends and relatives and went down to Chicago to face the grim years ahead.

What could she do? She tried running a rooming house, but she couldn't make expenses.

Then she tried selling hand-painted china that she had decorated herself; but no one wanted her sugar bowls and plates. Next, she tried to write songs; but publishers wouldn't buy them.

Fifteen years later, Carrie Jacobs Bond was to write "The End of a Perfect Day," a song that sold six million copies and netted her a quarter of a million dollars in cold cash.

But when she first started, she couldn't sell her songs for even five dollars apiece. Blighting poverty was her lot. Unable to pay her rent, she often feared that she would be put out on the street. In cold weather, she had to stay in bed to keep warm, for she couldn't burn more than two little bundles of kindling wood each day.

Finally, she became so poor she could eat only one meal a day; and second-hand dealers took away her furniture and silverware and gave her a little money that kept her from starving.

But during all this awful poverty and heartache, Carrie Bond continued to write beautiful songs—songs that would one day be sung around the world—songs like "Just A-Wearyin' For You" and "I Love You Truly."

Mrs. Bond wrote these songs on wrapping paper because she couldn't afford to buy writing paper, and she wrote by candle light because it was cheaper than gas light.

She wanted to advertise her songs, but she couldn't afford to buy space in a musical magazine, so she sewed dresses for the woman editor in order to pay for the cost of the advertisement.

At first, she found it difficult to get five dollars an evening for playing and singing her songs; but after she became known, Mrs. Frank J. Mackay, one of the social leaders of England, paid Carrie Bond one hundred dollars and her expenses to London and back in order to have her sing for only twelve minutes.

The first time Mrs. Bond tried to sing her songs in vaudeville, she was hissed off the stage. Heart-broken, she fled from the back door of the theater and ran up the street, hatless and coatless, with tears streaming down her cheeks; but years later, her name was featured in electric lights and she was paid a thousand dollars a week for singing in vaudeville.

On one occasion, she had an opportunity to give a concert before Governor Yates of Illinois. But she didn't have a dress that was fit to wear and she didn't have any money to buy one. So she dug down into an old trunk, pulled out some remnants and made herself a gown out of two lace curtains and a couple of yards of yellowed white satin.

Fifteen years ago, Mrs. Bond spent a day motoring with friends through the flower-laden drives of Southern California, past ivy-covered banks, and through hedges of exquisite Gold of Ophir roses. The day was glorified with a dreamy sort of happiness; and at eventide, she stood on the top of Mt. Rubidoux and watched the sinking sun splash the sky with all the gorgeous colors of a painting by the immortal Turner. As the great ball of burning gold slowly sank into the calm and mysterious Pacific, she said to herself, "Truly this has been a perfect day."

Words and phrases began forming in her mind. A song of praise and thanksgiving welled up in her heart; and while the spell was still hot upon her, she dashed off two stanzas of a poem. After a while she found herself humming a tune.

The thing was done.

A musical miracle had been performed. For, without effort, she had created a song that was destined to have a greater sale than any other piece of music since Gilbert and Sullivan had launched "Pinafore."

When Theodore Roosevelt was President, he invited Mrs. Bond to come to the White House and sing her songs for him.

When Harding was president, he did the same thing. "The End of a Perfect Day" was Warren Harding's favorite song, and he ordered the Marine Band always to play it as the closing number of their concerts.

> *When you come to the end of a perfect day,*
> *And you sit alone with your thought,*
> *While the chimes ring out with a carol gay,*
> *For the joy that the day has brought,*
> *Do you think what the end of a perfect day*
> *Can mean to a tired heart,*
> *When the sun goes down with a flaming ray,*
> *And the dear friends have to part?*
>
> *Well, this is the end of a perfect day,*
> *Near the end of a journey, too,*
> *But it leaves a thought that is big and strong,*
> *With a wish that is kind and true,*
> *For mem'ry has painted this perfect day*
> *With colors that never fade,*
> *And we find at the end of a perfect day,*
> *The soul of a friend we've made.*

## HE LOVES TO BE CALLED THE BIGGEST
## LIAR IN THE WORLD

Who do you suppose gets more mail than anyone else in the world? Clark Gable? No! Mae West? No! Rudy Valee? No!

I know a man who always get at least a million letters a year; and in 1932, he got three million letters from all parts of the world. That means more than eight thousand letters a day or twenty-eight letters while you are reading this one sentence.

Many of his correspondents call him ten kinds of a blankety-blank liar. He has been branded as a liar more often by more people than has anyone else who ever lived. And he loves it.

He has received letters without any name at all on the envelopes; they were merely addressed "To the Biggest Liar in the World," and, believe it or not, the Post Office delivered them to Robert L. Ripley!

Ripley makes a living by making people gasp. He made me gasp once when he showed me a letter written on a piece of human skin; and he made me gasp when he showed me a message that a man had written him on a single human hair. I couldn't believe it until I put the hair under a microscope and then I read the message just as plainly as if it had been written on a piece of paper. It said, "The finest welcome in the world to Robert L. Ripley."

Ripley told me that he once got a letter written in the

*Courtesy of Simon & Schuster*
### ROBERT L. RIPLEY
He's a walking encyclopedia—but he doesn't know his own telephone number

# ABOUT WELL KNOWN PEOPLE

Runic Code—the language used by the old Vikings thousands of years ago. He received another letter written in the secret service code used by the Confederate Spies during the Civil War.

One man from Ardara, Pennsylvania, wrote Ripley a message on a grain of rice. Think of it! Seven hundred and fifteen words, or two thousand, eight hundred and sixty letters on one grain of rice. Of course, you can't read these letters with the naked eye; but I read them very easily under a microscope.

He made me gasp again when he told me that the battle of Waterloo wasn't fought at Waterloo, that Pennsylvania was not named after William Penn and that Buffalo Bill never shot a buffalo.

He made me gasp when he said that if he killed me at midnight and every person who was told about it, told two other people within twelve minutes, everybody on earth would know it before morning.

One day Ripley said to me: "If you had fifteen guests at your house for dinner, how long would it take you to seat those fifteen guests in all possible ways?"

I did a bit of figuring, and I told him I thought I could arrange the seating in every possible way within a couple of hours.

He informed me that if I seated them differently, every minute, night and day, it would take almost two and a half million years to exhaust all the combinations. (And by that time, some of the guests would be too old to move.)

The story of Ripley's own life is almost as incredible as his cartoons.

His father was a carpenter and he warned Ripley that, if he became an artist, he would starve to death. The old man wanted his little boy to be a plumber or a bricklayer.

Ripley was "fired" from the first three newspapers on which he worked; yet he is making more money today than are the men who own the newspapers that "fired" him.

Ripley never studied drawing; yet he is the most widely imitated cartoonist in the world.

Ripley has traveled all over the world to visit the tombs of great men from Moah to Napoleon; but, believe it or not, he has never visited Grant's tomb, which is only three miles away from his apartment.

He is always running off to some far-off place like Kurdistan or Tanganyika; yet, believe it or not, he has been to his own office in New York only three times during the last six years. Why? Because he detests business details. He lets other people take care of that; and he does his drawing in a studio.

You ought to see that studio. Papers and books and drawings and affidavits and curios piled about in wild, hopeless confusion. I couldn't work in such disorder for a day. It would drive me crazy. But he is an artist, and he loves it—and he works all day in his pajamas.

Bob Ripley has always been intensely interested in sports. He wrote a book on Handball, and another on Boxing, and he started out in life to be a professional baseball player. He was signed up by the New York Giants; but he broke his arm while pitching; so he gave up baseball and started drawing sport cartoons.

One cold, December day in 1918—exactly one week before Christmas—he sat in his office trying to think of an idea for a cartoon. An hour or two slipped by. He couldn't think of a thing. The deadline was approaching.

# ABOUT WELL KNOWN PEOPLE

He had to draw something; so, in desperation, he picked up a few astonishing facts about athletics and made a cartoon which he called "Chumps and Champs." He didn't like the title, so he crossed it out and wrote "Believe It or Not."

That was the turning point of his life. One little idea on a dull, dreary afternoon, and presto!—he was on his way to a sensational, world-wide success. But it didn't come immediately.

He drew a "Believe It or Not" cartoon once a week for ten years; and, believe it or not, it attracted comparatively little attention. For ten years, his feature tottered on the verge of failure. As Rip once said to me, "You work and slave for ten years, and then become famous in ten minutes."

That is about what happened to him. For one day, in September, 1928, he drew a cartoon that startled a million readers.

He created a nation-wide furore when he said that Lindbergh was the sixty-seventh man to make a non-stop flight across the Atlantic Ocean. People rose up in indignation and demanded that he retract his impudent and insulting lie. But Ripley pointed out that Brown and Alcock had flown across the Atlantic years before Lindbergh was ever heard of—and so did the English dirigible R-34 with thirty-one men aboard; and so did the German dirigible ZR-3 with thirty-three men. So Lindbergh was really the sixty-seventh.

William Randolph Hearst saw that cartoon, and was entranced. So he insisted that Ripley draw a "Believe It or Not" cartoon for every one of his papers every day.

And Ripley started skyrocketing to fame.

The question that he is most often asked is how long he can keep his daily cartoon going without running out of material. He has enough material now to last him a life time. And at this minute, there are people all over the world writing him letters and sending him more amazing facts. Ripley told me he had a million people working for him.

Ripley probably knows more amazing facts than does anyone else in the world. Yet, believe it or not, he doesn't know the telephone number of his own office. I asked him for some information recently that necessitated his calling his office. He picked up the telephone and hemmed and hawed and hesitated and then had to call in his secretary in order to get his own telephone number.

# SHE DROVE A BATTERED OLD CAR INTO LOS ANGELES AND MADE A MILLION IN 18 MONTHS

Aimee Semple McPherson has probably received more front page newspaper publicity than has any other woman in the history of the world. Even an unimportant newspaper story about her has sent countless thousands rushing to the newsstands. A few years ago, a Los Angeles paper came out with the report that she had changed the color of her hair; and the circulation of that paper jumped three hundred per cent in one day.

The story of her life reads like a tale out of *The Arabian Nights*.

Legally, her name is Aimee Semple McPherson Hutton; but to her faithful followers, she is affectionately known as "Sister Aimee."

Born forty-three years ago in a tiny farmhouse near the little village of Ingersoll, in Ontaria, Canada, Sister Aimee, as a child, rode an old, white mare, called Flossie, five miles to school each day; she washed the dishes for her mother at night, milked the cows and taught the calves to drink by letting them suck her finger in a bucket of white, warm, foamy milk.

One Autumn, a poor, itinerant preacher by the name of Robert Semple drifted into the community. He had once been a boiler-maker by trade; and he put a boiler-maker's heat and fire into his preaching.

**AIMEE SEMPLE McPHERSON HUTTON**
At nineteen she was widowed, destitute, and stranded in China

"Sister Aimee" was only seventeen at the time; but she was converted, joined the church, married the boiler-maker evangelist and sailed away to China with him to convert the heathen.

Two years later, her husband died and left her penniless in China, with a child to support—and she was not yet twenty years old.

She took up a collection, returned to New York, and married a young grocery salesman, Robert McPherson, whom she met at a Salvation Army meeting.

Six years later, she divorced him, loaded her two children into a shabby car, and started West, stopping in almost every town she passed and calling on sinners to repent.

Sometimes she had to sleep in the car all night when it was mired down in a mud hole. Sometimes she and her children went hungry, and once they nearly froze to death in Colorado.

One evening, just at twilight, this amazing woman drove into Los Angeles, the City of the Angels, and started on her incredible career. She had no friends, no influence,—nothing but two hungry children, a battered old car and less than a hundred dollars in cash; yet within eighteen months, she was probably the most famous woman in California and she had a million dollars' worth of property.

She started preaching her gospel of joy, declaring the kingdom of Heaven was at hand; and huge crowds flocked to hear her. They overflowed the largest halls in Southern California. They crowded into vast boxing arenas, and finally, meetings were held outdoors, in wooded parks, and police reserves were despatched to handle the excited crowds.

Los Angeles went wild. The City of the Angels had

never known such a sensation. In a little more than a year, her shouting followers had built her the huge Angelus Temple, costing one and a half million dollars, and they had given it to her as her own property to do with as she wished.

In it, she had a silver band, larger and louder than any brass band Sousa ever had; she had an organ worthy of the Cathedral of Notre Dame; and she had a female choir larger and more beautiful than the Metropolitan Opera Chorus.

This great temple is packed with humanity an hour before the service starts; the doors are closed and hundreds are turned away. Under the magic spell of her mystic personality, sinners forsake their ways and the lame and the halt throw away their crutches and declare that they have been made whole. I have visited Sister Aimee's Temple, and I have seen the "miracle room" filled with the crutches, cots and wheel chairs discarded by those who have been healed by her magic influence.

On May 18, 1926, she went out to Ocean Park, put on her pea-green bathing suit, swam out into the Pacific Ocean and disappeared completely. Southern California was rocked by the news. It was a tremendous sensation. Her congregation moved out to the beach, built huge bon-fires and sang and wept and prayed, without ceasing, for thirty days and thirty nights. Fishermen dragged the waters for her body; deep sea divers explored the bottom of the ocean; and aviators searched for her from the sky. One diver died of exposure, a girl committed suicide, and others had to be forcibly restrained from drowning themselves in the sea. Such a religious frenzy had never been witnessed before on the Pacific coast. Newspapers all over the world

## ABOUT WELL KNOWN PEOPLE

featured the story. The Angelus Temple offered a reward of $25,000 for the return of Sister Aimee, dead or alive.

After being missing thirty-two days, she suddenly appeared at a lonely, little cabin on the edge of a tiny village in Mexico.

Where had she been? She declared that she had been held a prisoner during all that time. She said that when she came out of the ocean on May 18, a woman had pleaded with her to come and pray for her dying child. Sister Aimee went with her, was kidnapped, shoved into a car waiting behind a sand dune, and chloroformed. She claimed that she had been held for thirty-one days in a little shack in the desert. Then, one night, she crawled out of the hut, took a tomato can and cut the ropes that bound her. She said that she had wandered all that night and all the next day across the burning sands of the desert.

Many people refused to believe this sensational tale. They pointed out that if she had walked eighteen miles under a burning desert sun, she would have been sunburned; they pointed out that her clothes were in perfect condition, that her shoes weren't scuffed, that her hair was done up neatly in a hair net, and that she was not even thirsty, after walking eighteen miles across the hot, dry, sands.

She was dragged into court; and the best legal minds in California examined her and cross-examined her. She was baited, investigated, grilled, and denounced; but no one could ever shake her story.

Some people ridicule Sister Aimee; some adore her. But friend and foe alike all admit that she has accomplished an enormous amount of good, and that she is one of the most amazing women of the twentieth century.

*Courtesy of The News, New York*
UPTON SINCLAIR
**He has written more words than there are in both Old and New Testaments**

# THE MOST WIDELY READ LIVING AUTHOR WENT HUNGRY FOR YEARS

UPTON SINCLAIR has written forty-eight books and dashed off over five hundred pamphlets. Two million copies of his books have been sold in Germany, and three million in Russia. His radical novels probably helped to bring about the Russian Revolution. Although he is an American, his books are far more popular in Europe than they are here. I went into a little book store on the French Riviera one day and found more books by Upton Sinclair than I found by all other English and American authors put together. His books have been translated into forty-four languages, and Mr. Sinclair once told me that he didn't even know the names of some of these languages himself, nor where they are spoken. He is now the most widely read living author in all the world.

He is fifty-six years old, and he has been supporting himself by writing for forty years—ever since he was sixteen. He has written literally millions of words—more words than are found in both the Old and New Testaments.

He looks a bit like Woodrow Wilson and he is on fire with an ideal. He wants to end poverty, for he knows from experience how bitter poverty can be. He told me that at one time there was a period of six years during which he was seldom free from the gnawing pangs of hunger.

His father was a whisky salesman and a drunkard; and,

when he was a little boy in Baltimore, and later in New York, he used to go around at night from one saloon to another, looking for his father; then he would help him home and put him to bed, and his mother would take the money out of her drunken husband's pocket and hide it, so she could buy a little food the next day. They were so poor that they had to live in cheap, vermin-infested rooming houses on the Bowery—so poor that they had to move constantly from one grimy room to another because they couldn't pay their rent.

Upton Sinclair is a rabid prohibitionist, and who wouldn't be if whisky had wrecked his home and blighted his childhood as it did this boy's? He says that whisky shortened the lives of two of his closest friends, Jack London and Eugene V. Debs. Upton Sinclair doesn't even drink tea or coffee, and he doesn't smoke.

He never got a chance to go to school until he was ten years old; so he taught himself to read and, before he had ever seen the inside of a school, he had devoured all of Dickens and Thackeray, scores of other books, and a great deal of the encyclopedia. Two years after he started school, he was ready for high school.

When he entered college, he didn't have a dollar—and he had a mother to support. So he paid his way through the City College in New York and through Columbia University by selling jokes for a dollar a piece and by writing dime novels for cheap magazines. He dictated a story of eight thousand words every night. That meant that he was writing two average-sized novels every month —in addition to studying eight hours a day at Columbia. That is a gigantic performance. There isn't a man in a million who could do it.

## ABOUT WELL KNOWN PEOPLE

When he left college, he was making seventy a week by writing these wild, exciting tales for boys' magazines. That was a big income for an author who wasn't twenty years old. But Upton Sinclair wasn't interested in writing for money. He was driven by a desire to abolish poverty and injustice; so, in spite of the fact that he had a sickly wife and a child to support, he renounced all his income, set up a tent in New Jersey, and started writing novels of propaganda—novels to help reform the world. He spent five years turning out five novels; and these five books earned for him a thousand dollars—in other words, two hundred dollars a year, or less than sixty cents a day.

He suffered almost constantly from hunger. One day, his wife, craving a little luxury, went into a store and bought a red, checkered table cloth for thirty cents. But he made her return it and get the cash, for thirty cents meant a whole day's food supply for the family.

His sixth novel was *The Jungle*. It created a national sensation; and made thirty thousand dollars. He used all of it to finance a Utopian colony on the banks of the Hudson River, in New Jersey, a sort of a coöperative home, where writers and artists and musicians could live economically in congenial surroundings. Sinclair Lewis lived there for a while and tended the furnace; but he evidently didn't do a very good job for one night the house caught fire and burned to the ground—and that was the end of that.

Upton Sinclair has always been an ardent reformer. He and Inez Mullholland led the first woman suffrage parade in New York City. He has constantly fought for freedom of birth control; and he has been one of America's leading socialists for thirty years.

When he wants anything, he goes after it like a bulldog

after a cat. For example, he once decided to learn to play the violin. So he practised eight hours a day, almost every day, for three years. When the neighbors complained, he took his fiddle and went out in the woods and played to the birds and the squirrels.

He told me that he had been arrested four times. Once he was arrested in Wilmington, Delaware, and thrown into prison for eighteen hours because he was playing tennis on Sunday. He was arrested and put in the Tombs Prison in New York, for three days because he was walking up and down in front of John D. Rockefeller's office in silence. He was arrested for selling a copy of the Bible to the Boston police; and he was arrested for attempting to read the Constitution of the United States, while standing on private property, with the written permission of the owner.

# THE BIGGEST FAKER IN AMERICA WAS FOOLED AGAIN AND AGAIN

Who was the biggest faker in American history? The laurels undoubtedly belong to old P. T. Barnum, the Connecticut Yankee who made himself the most famous showman on earth.

Barnum was proud to call himself "The Prince of Humbugs." He even wrote a book entitled, *Humbugs of the World*, and was flattered when people denounced him as a fraud, a scoundrel, a mountebank, and a charlatan.

He loved to fool the public. He once advertised a strange horse, whose head was where its tail ought to be, and whose tail was where its head ought to be. The public flocked to behold this astonishing freak of nature; and, after paying twenty-five cents admission, they saw a horse backed into the stall, with his tail tied to the feed-trough.

On another occasion, he exhibited what he claimed was a real cherry-colored cat. The cat was black; but after getting the admission fee, Barnum said, "Yes, the cat is black, but so are lots of cherries."

Although Barnum's name is now a synonym for the circus, the fact is that he never organized what we now call a circus until he was sixty years of age; and he didn't form the Barnum & Bailey circus until he was seventy.

Barnum was right. He said there was a sucker born every minute, and he ought to have known, for although he made four million dollars out of exhibiting freaks and wild

P. T. BARNUM
There was one born every minute—including himself

animals, he occasionally proved to be a sucker himself.

For example, when he was a young man, he invested two thousand, five hundred dollars—which was all the money he had—in a concern manufacturing bears' grease. This magic preparation was supposed to grow hair on bald heads. Barnum's partner spent all the money, fled to Europe, and left Barnum with nothing but a recipe for making bears' grease.

Barnum once tried to sell illustrated copies of the Bible; but the agents that he hired swindled him out of every dollar he had.

On one occasion, he bought a patented fire extinguisher, but there was just one little thing wrong with it; it wouldn't put out fires. Finally, with unfaltering optimism, he became involved in the manufacture of clocks, was swindled out of half a million dollars, and was plunged into a bankruptcy that was a national sensation.

After losing every cent he had, he wrote a lecture entitled: "How to Make Money." He delivered that lecture even in the hushed and holy precincts of Oxford and Cambridge universities, and made as much as a thousand dollars a night out of it.

Barnum once raised a storm of indignation in England because he wanted to buy the house in which Shakespeare was born, take it apart, and bring it to America, piece by piece, to exhibit on Broadway.

In spite of all his bluster and "brass," the old showman suffered from moments of doubt and depression. He once sat down in his dismal hotel room, in Liverpool, England, and wept from discouragement and homesickness.

Barnum was a sincerely religious and pious man. He once heard a lecture on the evils of drunkenness; and although he had been a moderate drinker for twenty years, he rushed home and smashed all his champagne bottles, signed a pledge never to drink again, dashed out to the homes of his friends and persuaded twenty of them to sign the temperance pledge in one morning.

When Barnum was living in Bridgeport, Connecticut, he used to keep a white silk flag, with his initials on it, flying from the top of his house, so that his friends would know he was home. In order to get publicity for his museum and menagerie, Barnum used an elephant to plow a field on a farm near the railroad tracks, at Bridgeport. The keeper of the elephant was dressed up in red and yellow silk pantaloons, like an oriental potentate. And he was given a railroad time table and told to get busy plowing with his elephant whenever a train passed. Naturally, all the passengers rushed to the windows, agog with excitement. Newspapers all over America played up the story until it became the talk of the nation. Thousands of farmers wrote to Barnum wanting to buy elephants. He plowed the field fifty times in one summer, and got a hundred thousand dollars' worth of free publicity.

Barnum wrote the story of his own life in 1855 and kept revising and republishing it for thirty-five years. He bought a million copies of his autobiography, paid nine cents a copy for the book and sold it for a dollar.

One day, he nailed a large packing box to the wall of his office in Bridgeport, where he kept the winter quarters for his circus. He painted these words in huge, black letters across the box: "NOT TO BE OPENED UNTIL AFTER THE DEATH OF P. T. BARNUM."

The box created a lot of excitement. His employees hoped that he was leaving them a fortune. However, when

## ABOUT WELL KNOWN PEOPLE

the box was opened, it was found to be filled with copies of his book entitled, *The Life of P. T. Barnum, Written by Himself*. He ordered that a copy of the book be given to all of his oldest employees.

Barnum had no sons to carry on the name of which he was so proud; so he offered to give his grandson, C. H. Seeley, an additional $25,000 provided he would call himself "Barnum Seeley."

When Barnum was near death, the *Evening Sun*, of New York, asked the great showman's publicity agent if Barnum would object to having his obituary published before he died. The publicity man said, "No, go ahead. The old man will be delighted."

So the next day Barnum read four columns about his own death, and he loved it.

When he died, the newspapers of America gave more space to the story of his career than had ever been given to any man except a president of the United States. How that would have pleased the venerable showman, if he had only known it!

The last words he ever uttered were a request to know how much money the Barnum and Bailey Circus had taken in that day at Madison Square Garden.

VILHJALMUR STEFANSSON
Big bad wolves are his meat

# THE MAN WHO ATE SHOESTRINGS—AND LIKED THEM

I ONCE talked for three hours with a man who had spent eleven years up beyond the Arctic Circle; and during six years of that time, he had lived on nothing but meat and water. The man is Stefansson—a splendid, blonde Norseman, with the blood of the old Vikings coursing through his veins.

Stefansson was the first explorer in the world who ever dared to venture out on the desolate ice of the Arctic Ocean, without food or fuel, and try to live on the game that he shot.

When he first suggested such a thing, the experts told him he was crazy, and the Eskimos warned him that he would starve to death. But would he? He wasn't so sure. He was a scientist and he wanted the facts. So he and two of his companions took guns and ammunition and went out and lived for months on cakes of ice, floating around in the Arctic Ocean.

Some of these cakes of ice were no larger than a football, and some were as big as the State of Rhode Island. Some of the ice was only a few inches thick; some of it was a hundred feet thick. And all of it was drifting about in an ocean that was from one to three miles deep.

During the first forty days on the ice, they ate all the food they had brought with them. From that time on, they ate nothing except the seals and polar bears that they shot. How did they get their drinking water? Well, they made a fire out of blubber, which is the fat found on seals; and with this fire, they melted sea ice and got fresh water.

And here is the astonishing part of the story: Stefansson and his men traveled seven hundred miles over the shifting ice, and instead of dying from starvation, as the experts had said they would, they gained several pounds and didn't miss a single meal in ninety-seven days!

Stefansson said they would have died if they had eaten nothing but lean meat, but they were all right so long as they ate all the fat meat they wanted, along with the lean.

Sometimes they ate their meat raw, but they usually cooked it, using blubber for fuel. Sometimes they cut the hair off a bearhide and used the hair for fuel.

On one trip, one of Stefansson's men exhausted his supply of tobacco. He got so hungry for tobacco that he chewed the cloth in which he had been carrying it; and he even broke up his pipe and chewed pieces of that.

Most explorers carry their food on dog sledges, and have to eat sparingly and they usually lose many of their dogs by starvation. But Stefansson lived by shooting game; and during all the eleven years he was exploring the Arctic, he never had even one dog starve to death. In fact, his dogs seldom knew what hunger meant.

Who's afraid of the big, bad wolf? Well, Stefansson isn't. He says he has eaten dozens of big, bad wolves. He said he would rather have a nice piece of roast wolf than roast veal.

Stefansson told me that his men tried eating wild ducks, wild geese, partridges and owls. Then they took a vote on which one they liked best, and most of them said they would rather have owl than wild ducks or partridges. He

## ABOUT WELL KNOWN PEOPLE

himself has even eaten the rawhide strings on his snow shoes. He believes that a piece of boiled, fresh rawhide isn't bad; it tastes something like pigs' feet. He says it is a good idea to wear skin clothing in the Far North instead of woolen clothes; because if you get too hungry, you can eat your rawhide clothes.

So if you've got an old rawhide boot around the house, you had better keep it. You can never tell what may happen.

When Stefansson came back to New York and told about living for years on nothing but meat, some of the best known diet experts denounced him as seven kinds of a compound liar. They said it couldn't be done. So, in the interests of science, Stefansson and one of his companions agreed to live on nothing but meat and water, for a whole year, right in the heart of New York, while going about their business as usual. The experiment was carried out scientifically under the auspices of the Cornell University Medical School and the Russell Sage Institute, located in Bellevue Hospital.

This experiment lasted twelve months—and during all that time, the men were constantly given the most rigid and searching tests known to medical science. Their blood was analyzed, time after time. Their blood pressure was taken every week. Even the air that came out of their lungs was analyzed. And what were the results? Well, there were no bad effects whatever. While eating nothing but meat, they stood the scorching summer heat of New York better than usual. When Stefansson's companion, Anderson, started the experiment, he had high blood pressure, his hair was falling out and he was constantly subject to head colds; but in ninety days after he started his all-meat diet, his blood pressure became normal and remained normal, his hair stopped falling out and he had fewer colds than usual.

During all that time, he and Stefansson had practically no tooth decay at all. Stefansson told me that the only communities that are absolutely free from tooth decay are Eskimo villages where the people eat nothing but meat ninety-nine per cent of the time. And he said that as soon as these Eskinmos start eating the kind of food that we eat, their teeth begin to decay like ours.

# HE DREAMED OF PUNCHING COWS WHILE YANKING TEETH

Zane Grey battled his way up from discouragement and poverty to the position of being one of the most widely read novelists on this planet. And he did it while living in the little village of Lackawaxen, Pennsylvania, on the banks of the Delaware River.

Editors have frequently paid Zane Grey $75,000 for only the magazine rights to a story, even before the story was written; yet he couldn't sell his first few books for seventy-five cents. His publishers tell me that they have sold more than a million copies of Zane Grey's books each year, for three successive years; but when he started writing, he was such a failure that he went cold and hungry.

His father insisted that he study dentistry. Zane Grey had no more desire to be a dentist than he had to be a coal miner. But orders were orders; so this man, who was destined to become world-famous as a story teller of two-gun men and cattle thieves, studied dentistry, opened an office in New York, and spent years of his life filling people's teeth. But his heart wasn't in his work.

While his hands were busy grinding molars, his mind was out West with the riders of the purple sage. If a horse trotted over the cobble stones under his window, he instantly thought of mail robbers and the pony express.

As the years went by, Zane Grey found himself face to face with a daily tragedy. He despised his profession. He had to whip and drive himself to go to his office every

*Courtesy of Harper Brothers*
ZANE GREY
His fingers were numb with cold as he wrote

morning, like a galley slave scourged to his dungeon. The only happiness that he found in life was in his day dreams.

So, determining to become a writer, he abandoned his profession and moved to Lackawaxen, where he could live economically and hunt and fish while he was learning to write.

He would toil and struggle for months, sometimes for a whole year over a story, writing and revising, changing the plot, altering the characters. Then, when he had finished a tale, he would read it through, from beginning to end, read it with a wild rush of enthusiasm. It sounded magnificent. He believed he was on the verge of becoming a great author. But no one else believed it. In all New York City, there wasn't a single publisher who wanted his stories.

He devoted all his time, for five long years, to writing stories—and his income during those five years was absolutely zero. He made a little money occasionally by playing professional baseball in the summer time, but he made nothing from his writing.

One day, when he was in New York, trying to sell a story, he met Colonel Buffalo Jones. Colonel Jones wanted someone with a flair for words to go out West with him and write about the trip. It was the first encouragement Zane Grey had had. He jumped at the chance, his heart thrilling at the prospect of a real adventure.

After spending six months among the cowboys and wild horses of the west, he came back home and wrote a novel entitled *The Last of the Plainsmen*. This time he was positive he had a winner. So he sent his manuscript to the publishing house of Harper—and waited two weeks. Unable to endure the suspense any longer, he hurried to New York and called on the publishers.

They handed him his manuscript and said, "We are sorry; but there is nothing in this story to convince us that you can ever write fiction." He was absolutely crushed. He was dazed. This was the fifth book they had rejected. He couldn't have been more stunned if someone had hit him over the head with a club. Reeling down the stairs, he grabbed a lamp post to keep from falling; and with his manuscript under his arm, he leaned against that lamp post, and wept.

He returned home, beaten and crushed. He had been living on a little money his wife had; but that had practically all melted away by the end of five years, and they had a baby to support. They were desperate. But his wife encouraged him to write still another novel. It was in the dead of winter. The tiny stove wasn't large enough to heat the room, and his fingers grew numb with cold as he wrote. He had to stop every few minutes and open the stove door and thrust his hands in close to the flames to get them warm.

All through that winter, and far into the next summer, he toiled over that story; and when it was finished, the publishing house of Harper again turned their thumbs down. Frantic with despair, Zane Grey pleaded with the editor to take the manuscript home and read it himself. Two days later, Zane Grey returned, and the editor was all smiles. He said, "My wife sat up last night until almost daybreak reading your story. She thinks it's great. And so we're going to publish it."

The title of that book was *Heritage of the Desert*. It was an immediate and immense success.

At last, after years of poverty and failure, Zane Grey was on his way to become one of the biggest money-making writers, and one of the most popular novelists in America. For, since that time, he has published fifty-four books, and more than fifteen million copies have been sold in the United States alone.

MRS. ABRAHAM LINCOLN
She prided herself on her table manners

## MRS. LINCOLN FLUNG HOT COFFEE IN ABRAHAM'S FACE

ALMOST a century ago, Abraham Lincoln and Mary Todd were married, in Springfield, Illinois, and their marriage proved to be of the most unfortunate and unhappy unions in the history of this nation.

The only comment that Lincoln ever made, in writing about his marriage, was a postscript that he added to a business letter, written a week after the event. The letter was written to Samuel Marshal, and it is now in the possession of the Chicago Historical Society. In it Lincoln says, "There is no news here except my marriage, which to me is a matter of profound wonder."

William H. Herndon was Lincoln's law partner for a fifth of a century, and Herndon knew Lincoln better than any other man ever knew him; and Herndon said, "If Lincoln ever had a happy day in twenty years, I never knew of it. And Herndon thought that Lincoln's marriage had a lot to do with his sadness.

I once spent three years writing a biography of Lincoln, and while I was writing it, I believe I made as careful a study of the home life of the Lincoln family as it is possible for anyone to make. I carefully examined and re-examined every shred of evidence that is in existence; and I came to the reluctant and painful conclusion that the greatest tragedy in Abraham Lincoln's life was his marriage.

Shortly after he and Mary Todd were engaged, Lincoln

began to realize that they were exact opposites, in every way, and that they could never be happy. They were the exact opposites in temperament, in tastes, in training, and desires.

For example, Mary Todd had attended a snobbish finishing school in Kentucky; she spoke French with a Parisian accent, and was one of the best educated women in Illinois. But Lincoln had attended school a total of less than twelve months in his entire life.

She was extremely proud of her family. Her grandfathers and great grandfathers and great uncles had been generals and governors, and one had been Secretary of the Navy.

But Lincoln had no pride whatever in his family tree. He said that only one of his relatives had ever visited him while he lived in Springfield, and that that one was accused of stealing a jew's-harp before he got out of town.

Mary Todd was deeply interested in dress and show and ostentation. But Lincoln took no interest whatever in his appearance. In fact, he would sometimes walk down the street with one trouser leg on the outside of his boot and the other trouser leg stuffed in the inside his boot.

Mary had been taught that good table manners were almost a sacred rite; but Lincoln had been reared in a log cabin with a dirt floor, and he stuck his own knife into the butter plate and did a score of things that shocked Mary and almost drove her wild.

She was proud and haughty. He was humble and democratic. She was intensely jealous; and created a scene if he merely looked at another woman. Her jealousy was so bitter and so unreasoning and so fantastic that it makes one gasp to read about it even now.

## ABOUT WELL KNOWN PEOPLE

Shortly after they were engaged, Lincoln wrote her a letter saying that he didn't love her sufficiently to marry her. He gave this letter to his friend, Joshua Speed, and asked Speed to give it to Mary Todd. Speed tore up the letter, threw it in the fire and told Lincoln to go and see Mary Todd himself. He did, and when he told her that he didn't want to marry her, she started to cry. Lincoln could never stand seeing a woman cry; so he took her in his arms and kissed her and said he was sorry.

The wedding day was set for January 1, 1841. The wedding cake was baked, the guests were assembled, the preacher was there, but Lincoln didn't appear. Why? Well, Mary Todd's sister afterwards explained it by saying that Lincoln went crazy. And her husband added: "Yes, crazy as a loon." The fact is that he did become ill—dangerously ill in body and ill in mind, and he sank into a spell of melancholy so deep and so terrible that it almost unbalanced his reason. His friends found him at daylight, mumbling incoherent sentences. He said he didn't want to live. He wrote a poem on suicide and had it published in one of the Springfield papers, and his friends took his knife away from him, to keep him from killing himself.

Lincoln then wrote the most pitiful letter of his life. It was written to his law partner who was then in Congress. This is the letter, word for word:

> I am now the most miserable man living. If what I feel were equally distributed to the whole human family, there would not be one cheerful face on earth. Whether I shall ever be any better, I cannot tell. I awfully forbode that I shall not. To remain as I am is impossible. I must die or be better it seems to me.

For almost two years after that, Lincoln had nothing whatever to do with Mary Todd. Then a self-appointed matchmaker in Springfield brought them together, behind closed doors, and Mary Todd told Lincoln it was his duty to marry her. And he did.

While I was out in Illinois, writing that book about Lincoln, I went to see Uncle Jimmy Miles, a farmer who lives near Springfield. One of his uncles was Herndon, Lincoln's law partner; and one of his aunts ran a boarding house where Mr. and Mrs. Lincoln came to live shortly after they were married. Uncle Jimmy Miles told me that he had often heard his aunt tell this story: One morning, Mr. and Mrs. Lincoln were having breakfast with the rest of the boarders, and Lincoln said something that displeased his wife; so she picked up a cup of hot coffee and dashed it into his face, and she did it in the presence of the other boarders. Lincoln didn't answer her. He didn't scold her. He said nothing, while the landlady brought a wet cloth and wiped off his face and his clothes. Similar incidents probably occurred in the Lincoln household for years.

But let us not judge Mrs. Lincoln too harshly. She finally went insane; and perhaps much earlier her mind was being affected by oncoming insanity.

One of the most beautiful things I know about Abraham Lincoln is the fact that he endured his unhappy home life for twenty-three years without bitterness, without resentment and without saying a word about it to anyone. He endured it with Christ-like forgiveness, and with a patience that was almost divine.

# HE HATES CROWDS BUT HE HAS AN AUDI-ENCE OF 20,000,000 PEOPLE A DAY

For sixteen years, O. O. McIntyre has been writing a column entitled "New York Day by Day." Four hundred and ninety-eight newspapers print it, and about twenty million people read it daily.

He is the most celebrated commentator on New York life that the old town has ever known; and yet he was born out in Missouri and never saw New York until he was thirty-four.

To millions of people, Oscar Odd McIntyre—or "Odd" as his friends call him—is the most famous person in New York.

I was down in Amarillo, Texas, a few years ago, and I found that folks down there talked about only two people in New York—O. O. McIntyre and Arthur Brisbane.

You can paste one of Odd McIntyre's pictures on an envelope and drop it in a letter box without any name or address on it, and it will be delivered to his Park Avenue apartment. He gets at least one such letter each week.

There are a lot of odd things about Odd McIntyre. For example, he is paid $2,150 per week for writing his daily column; yet he has never talked, face to face, more than three times in his life with the man who pays him that salary.

He makes more than $100,000 a year by writing; yet

O. O. MCINTYRE
You can paste his picture on an envelope and he'll get it

he doesn't have a stenographer. He pecks it all out himself on a portable typewriter.

His salary is more than that of the president of the United States; yet he doesn't know what his office looks like. He has an office, but he has never been near it; he does all his work at home.

Odd McIntyre hasn't the slightest desire to go on the air, though he was offered thirty-one radio contracts last year. One concern agreed to put a microphone right in his New York apartment and pay him five hundred dollars a minute for talking in front of it; but he wouldn't do it. He said he got goose pimples at the very thought of it.

He doesn't want to appear in the movies, in spite of the fact that Hollywood has been hot on his track for years. Warner Brothers were determined to have him act as master of ceremonies in one of their films. They tried to tempt him with one offer after another, but he kept saying, "No. No." Finally, they sent him a blank contract saying, "Write your own figure—anything you want—and sign it and send it back."

He sent it back all right, but it didn't have his signature.

I asked him why he turned down these fabulous offers, and he said, "Well, because I don't know how to talk." He told me he tried to make a speech once, at a dinner given for Jack Dempsey in Los Angeles; and when he stood up, he was so scared that he swallowed and stammered and couldn't say a word.

He said that if he tried to talk on the radio or appear in pictures, he might be an awful flop. "Besides," he added, "what would be the use, anyway, for the Government would take eighty cents of each dollar that I made, for income tax."

Odd McIntyre was born out in Plattsburg, Missouri, where his father ran a hotel. His mother died when he was three years old; and so he was reared by his grandmother, in Gallipolis, Ohio. I had often wondered how and why this small town boy ever came to be the voice of Broadway and he told me how it happened.

I'll quote his own words. He said, "Well, when I was just a kid out in Gallipolis, a traveling eye doctor from New York used to stop in our town and fit my grandmother with glasses. This fellow sported a high silk hat and a cutaway coat. By George! I thought he was grand. I stared at him until I was pop-eyed. I remember that he was the first man I ever saw who wore a white edging on the inside of his vest."

Later on, Odd McIntyre worked as a night clerk in the hotel in Gallipolis, and there he saw traveling men from New York—men who wore spats and talked about Broadway with a knowing air. This country boy was tremendously impressed by all this glamour; so he resolved to travel himself.

He had no money and no "pull," but he had youth and the fire of ambition in his heart. He read all the books he could find about New York; and, after working on newspapers in Ohio for several years, he came to Manhattan and took a position on *Hampton's* magazine. Three months after he landed in town, the magazine failed. He then got a position as copy reader and make-up man on the *Evening Mail*; but he was sickly and incompetent—and so he was fired.

Then he started to do the thing he had always wanted to do. He began writing a daily piece about New York. But nobody wanted to publish it; so, in order to get a start, he gave it away to newspapers, until he created a demand for his work.

He was so weak, from a nervous break-down, that he could write only for a little while at a time. Then he would have to go to bed, rest for an hour or two, and then get up and write again. His health, however, is top-notch today.

Here is a strange thing about O. O. McIntyre—although he lives in one of the most densely populated cities on earth, he has always had a haunting fear of crowds.

For one whole year, he absolutely refused to leave his hotel. He had a hat and a cane and his friends could get him to go as far as the front door; but nothing would induce him to step onto the sidewalk. It seemed as if there were an invisible hand holding him back.

The psychologists have a word for this emotional affliction. They call it a "crowd phobia." Odd McIntyre told me that, for years, he wouldn't go to the theatre unless he had a seat on the aisle; and he said that he would be frightened even now if he found himself alone in the midst of a large crowd in Madison Square Garden.

Odd McIntyre, the typical man about town, doesn't drink and doesn't smoke. The only thing he offered me was a package of chewing gum. He has a Rolls Royce and a chauffeur. Yet his favorite exercise is walking, and he manages to cover at least three miles every day.

He has his clothes made by Lanvin, the Paris dressmaker; and he has a wardrobe that would rival the sartorial trappings of the Prince of Wales; yet he sits around all day writing in his dressing gown and lounging pajamas.

He never had but one sweetheart—and he married her

twenty-six years ago. He calls her "Snooks" and she calls him "Lover."

Will Rogers is his favorite movie actor. His favorite book is *Of Human Bondage* by Somerset Maugham, and his favorite musical selection is *The Song of India*.

# CHRIST WAS NOT BORN ON CHRISTMAS DAY

About three hundred years ago, when New England was a far-removed colony of the British Crown, the wife of a village squire in Hadley, Massachusetts, walked across the fields one December day and visited a German lady who was celebrating Christmas. This German lady had cut down a small pine tree in the forest, dragged it home through the snow, lighted it with candles, and her children were dancing around it, singing Christmas carols. Nothing wrong with that, was there?

Yet the grim-faced, Puritan fathers, who ruled New England then, hauled this woman before a council of village elders, thundered at her, denounced her, and threw her out of the Church, bag and baggage. And back in those days, that was tantamount to social ostracism.

What had she done? She had committed the heathen sin of celebrating Christmas. The old Puritans despised Christmas. With wrathful voices, they denounced it from their pulpits. They branded it as an unholy pagan holiday and declared it was an insult to God. They even passed a law which heaped fines and public disgrace upon anyone who attempted to celebrate Christmas.

When the fiery-tempered Cromwell and his singing soldiers climbed up into the seats of the mighty in Merrie England, they too passed laws abolishing the pagan holiday called Christmas.

Why all this cry and uproar against the celebration of

**MERRY OLD SANTA CLAUS**
Three hundred years ago he was Public Enemy No. 1

Christmas? For one thing, the old Puritans knew that Christ was not born on Christmas day.

Scholars were wrangling about the date of Christ's birth less than two hundred years after he died. Some claimed that he was born on May 20th—others contended that the correct date was April 19th. Still others denounced these dates as superstitions, and declared he was born on November 17th. Modern scholars confess that we haven't the remotest idea about the exact time of the birth of Jesus.

Even in Bethlehem, where Christ was born, Christmas will be celebrated this year at three different times. One group celebrates it on December 25th, another on January 6th, and still another sect on January 18th. In Abyssinia, Christmas is celebrated every month of the year, except March. Christ was *not* born 1934 years ago, but 1939 years ago. How come?

Well, we didn't begin to reckon time from the birth of Christ until eight hundred years after his death. Then the crude scholars of that far-off day made a mistake of five years in their figures.

For thousands of years, the Romans, gorged with food, and drunk with wine, celebrated the feast of Saturnalia in December. Saturn was their god of Agriculture, and after they had gathered their crops for the season, they held high festival in his honor, decorating their houses with evergreen and holly, giving dolls to their children, and showering gifts upon one another.

Centuries ago, old bald-headed Constantine rose up in the Roman Senate, straightened his gay-colored wig, and decreed that Christianity was the official religion of the Roman Empire. And when he did that, he ordered the Christians to celebrate the birth of Christ during the feast of Saturn, so he merged the two festivals into one.

Many curious and colorful superstitions have grown up around Christmas. Old women, pop-eyed with strange beliefs, declare that when the clock strikes midnight on Christmas Eve, the bees sing the 100th Psalm, and they say that the sheep open their mouths and bleat the word "Bethlehem."

One of my secretaries was raised in Louisiana, and she tells me that the negroes taught her that the cows literally get down on their knees and talk to one another on Christmas Eve. Well, maybe they do, down in Louisiana; but I was once a cowboy myself out in South Dakota; and if the cows out west ever talked on Christmas Eve, it must have been in hog Latin or pidgin English, for I couldn't understand them.

However, over in Norway, the farmers give their cattle a tub of home-brewed ale on Christmas Eve—and those critters not only talk—they lean up against the lamp posts and sing "Sweet Adeline!"

Old Santa Claus, who is coming down your chimney on Christmas Eve, in his pagan youth was the fire-god of ancient peoples. He brought presents to the children in Rome thousands of years ago—and he comes with his reindeer and jingle bells from the far North; for, like all the gods of our tribal fathers, he lives in the twinkling firmament around the North Star.

Christmas may have been a pagan orgy thousands of years ago—but who cares? Today, it is the most happy and universal holiday in all the western world.

## THE GRAND DUCHESS WHO MARRIED SO SHE COULD WEAR SILK STOCKINGS

It was my privilege, not long ago, to be a guest in the home of a princess—the Grand Duchess Marie, of Russia. Her uncle was Alexander the third, Czar of Russia. Her cousin was Nicholas the second, the last Czar of Russia; and her playmates were the daughters of the Czar of Russia. She is probably the most famous royal personage in the Western Hemisphere.

I wondered what she would be like. Would she be beautiful and full of charm and personality? Would she be friendly and democratic or would she be aloof and cold?

Well, I found her to be exquisite and friendly and charming.

She told me an astonishing thing about herself; she is now in her early forties, and she said that during the first half of her life, she had been timid and shy and that she had suffered severely from an inferiority complex.

Born into the wealth and glamour of the mighty Romanoff family that had ruled Russia for three hundred years, she was so important that, even as a child, she rode in a golden coach, drawn by three pairs of white horses, and surrounded by mounted hussars in scarlet uniforms.

And she was so famous that crowds would gather on the sidewalks and stand for an hour for the privilege of catching but a glimpse of her royal highness as she passed by. Yet she, a princess, a Grand Duchess of Russia, suffered

Courtesy of Viking Press
GRAND DUCHESS MARIE
She wasn't permitted to drop even a crumb

# ABOUT WELL KNOWN PEOPLE

acutely from an inferiority complex. Sounds incredible, doesn't it?

Her childhood training had a lot to do with it. She never knew a mother's love, for her mother died when she was a year and a half old; and her father married a second time, and this time, he married a woman who was not of royal blood, so he was banished from Russia and his property was taken away from him. So the little princess was brought up very largely by strangers—by nurses and governesses and teachers.

This royal princess of Russia, could hardly speak a word of Russian when she was six years old. Up to that time, she had been taught nothing but English; and it was not good English, either. She dropped her "h's" and said "appy" instead of "happy" just as her English nurses did.

Her tutors kept her in ignorance of the power and prestige that were hers by right of royal birth; and since sons of the royal family in the past had aroused bitter resentment by being too arrogant, her teachers were ordered to put humility into her little soul. And they did, all right.

She told me that she was reared in the most "rigorous simplicity." Those were her exact words—"rigorous simplicity." She said that if she had wasted a piece of bread as big as her thumb-nail, she would have been punished for it. If she dropped a crumb on the floor, she had to pick it up and put it back on the table. And her food was very simple and very plain. Frequently, she had nothing but bread and milk for supper.

Her clothes were extremely plain, too. Although she lived among paintings and works of art that were priceless, and although the royal family of Russia was worth hundreds of millions of dollars, nevertheless, this princess wore cotton dresses and cotton gloves and cotton stockings right up to the time of her marriage. In fact, she told me that one reason why she wanted to marry was the hope that she could have silk stockings after she was married.

Later in life, she lived with her aunt and uncle. Her aunt was jealous of her and resented her presence in the house. If she was only sixty seconds late for a meal, her aunt punished her and she also punished her if she failed to carry on an interesting conversation with the guests. Her aunt wouldn't even let the child laugh in her presence, because she thought childish laughter was shocking and common.

The princess told me that she never knew what a real home was; that her childhood was sad and lonely, and that her grandmother, Queen Olga of Greece, was the only person in the world who gave her any real appreciation of what warm love and maternal tenderness could be. Marie was so hungry for affection that she wanted to fling herself into her grandmother's arms; but she said, "I was so little used to caresses that I did not know how to begin."

When she was sixteen, she wanted a mandolin; but she didn't have the money to buy it and she didn't have the courage to ask her uncle for it. She was afraid he would refuse her. So she got one of her teachers to ask her uncle if she could have a mandolin.

Her uncle said "Yes"—and that was the last word he ever did say, for a few seconds later, an anarchist threw a bomb and blew his body into bits.

# THE MAN WHO WAS SWEPT OUT TO SEA ON AN ICE-FLOE

ONE of the happiest men on earth is Doctor Grenfell, of Labrador. His hair is grey, his eyes are tired, and his hands are rough from frost-bite and arctic winds. He has been shipwrecked four different times among the icebergs, and has slept all night on the floating ice. He has been lost in the wilds of Labrador and almost frozen to death. He has been so hungry that he even ate the sealskin straps off his boots.

He is past seventy, and he hasn't any money.

But don't feel sorry for Doctor Grenfell, of Labrador. I don't, I envy him; for he has found about the only thing that matters in the world—happiness and contentment.

Forty-five years ago, Doctor Grenfell was graduated from Oxford and opened his office in the ultra-fashionable Mayfair section of London. His practice grew, he prospered, and he was apparently headed for big things in England; but he needed a rest. So he decided to spend a summer vacation among the fishermen of Labrador.

Labrador is a cold, inhospitable country, stretching fifteen hundred miles along the Eastern coast of Canada from Newfoundland in the South to the Hudson Straits in the North. For nine months out of each year, the unhappy land is covered with snow and ice, and the ground is frozen until the first of July. The country is barren, and the fishermen often feed their hungry cows on salt codfish and the tails of whales.

**SIR WILFRED GRENFELL**
Thirty thousand fishermen tell him their symptoms

Dr. Grenfell was astonished to find that there was not one physician to care for the thirty thousand fishermen inhabiting this bleak and frosty coast.

He did what he could for them that summer; and, in the autumn, he returned to London. But prescribing pills for his rich patients in fashionable Mayfair seemed trifling and inconsequential. He had caught a vision. The North was calling him. So back he went, and for forty-two years now, he has been sailing up and down the treacherous coasts of Labrador; and has made himself the best-loved physician in all the world. King George of England knighted him for his unselfish and heroic services.

Doctor Grenfell recently talked to me for hours about his extraordinary experiences. Once he called to see an old woman who had fallen on the ice and crushed her leg. Infection had set in, and her leg had to be amputated. But the pious old woman, nurtured on the precepts of the Old Testament, refused to take chloroform. She believed God had sent her the pain and that it was her Christian duty to bear it. Nothing less than a load of dynamite could have changed her mind.

So she had her five grown sons sit on her and hold her down while Doctor Grenfell cut off her leg. She didn't whimper; but the Doctor told me that the experience almost wrecked him.

People often send Doctor Grenfell books and clothing to be given away in Labrador. He once got a barrel of spats. Imagine those two-fisted old cod fishermen wearing spats! Another box contained a red hunting coat and a silk hat. And someone sent an elegant book of etiquette that was almost a hundred years old. The book was torn apart and pasted on a shack for wall paper; so the old salt that lives in that cabin can look at the wall now during the long winter nights and read what was being done in polite society a century ago.

These Labrador fishermen are very superstitious, very religious and often very hungry. Doctor Grenfell once found an isolated village where the people were on the verge of starvation—for weeks they had eaten nothing but a paste, made of flour and water. Yet they refused to eat their pigs. Why? Because the pigs had broken into the church and eaten a Bible. So they felt that the pigs were holy, that they had God in them, and must not be touched.

The most exciting experience of Doctor Grenfell's life occurred on Easter Sunday, in 1908. An emergency call came from a man sixty miles away. The poor fellow was in agony, and would soon be dead unless he could be operated upon. So Doctor Grenfell harnessed his dogs and set out with his sled, racing against death. To save time, he took a short cut across the floating ice in the bay. Suddenly the wind changed. The ice started drifting out to sea. The situation was desperate. The dogs made a mad dash for shore. But it was too late. The soft ice gave way, and they plunged into the frigid water. Doctor Grenfell grabbed his knife and cut the dogs loose from the sled. The sled sank, but he and the dogs swam to a floating cake of ice. Doctor Grenfell lost all his warm clothes when the sled sank. The few clothes that he had on were of no use for they were soaking wet with ice water. A bitter wind was blowing and night was coming on. He felt himself growing numb with cold. He was drowsy. He knew he was freezing to death.

There was only one way out. So he took his pocket knife and killed three of his dogs. Piling up the dead bodies of the dogs to act as a wind break, he wrapped their furry skins about his shivering body and lay down and slept all night on the ice pan that was rocking about in the sea. When morning came, he took the bones of his dogs, tied them together to make a pole, tied his shirt to the end of the pole, and then waved it frantically, hour after hour, at the lonely cliffs on the shore. It seemed utterly hopeless. He was a long way out, and he knew there wasn't one chance in a thousand of his ever being seen.

Suddenly, he thought he saw the flash of an oar in the bright morning sunlight. No! It wasn't possible. Surely his eyes must be playing tricks. Then he saw the flash again. Yes, it was an oar! A boat was fighting its way through the ice and he was saved.

What an experience, and what a man!

When I said as much to Doctor Grenfell, he protested.

"Come now," he said, "you mustn't try to make a martyr of me. It has all been jolly good fun, you know."

*Courtesy of Ladies Home Journal*
LOUISA MAY ALCOTT
The best people said she'd come to no good end

## A GREAT AUTHOR WHO WAS BORED BY HER OWN MASTERPIECE

FIVE hundred years before the birth of Christ, Aeschylus the Greek dramatist presented his immortal tragedies in Athens; but never, from the far-off days of Aeschylus to the record-smashing times of *Abie's Irish Rose,* has any other theatrical attraction ever equalled the three weeks record of the moving picture version of *Little Women,* at "Radio City" in New York.

On the seventeenth day of its run, the demand for seats was so great that people stood in a long line that extended for several blocks. Shoppers, bent on their Christmas errands, looked on in astonishment. Such a sight had never been witnessed before in the history of New York.

The story of how this sentimental masterpiece was written is an astonishing tale in itself.

In her youth, Louisa M. Alcott had been a whistling tomboy. Even when she grew up, she had no interest whatever in girls and she didn't want to write about girls. But her publisher insisted that she write a girl's story. She consented, but inwardly she rebelled.

Now, it is almost an axiom among writers that unless the author himself feels joy in writing his tale, no one will find joy in reading it.

Yet, Louisa Alcott found no happiness whatever in writing *Little Women.* In fact, it bored her, bored her until she could hardly stand it. She repeatedly threw down her pencil and paper, whistled for her dog, and went bounding off through the woods. On other days, she tossed her manuscript aside and hurried across the town to argue with her friend, Ralph Waldo Emerson.

When she had finished *Little Women*, she thought she had written a failure. But it immediately became a "best seller," and has remained a "best seller," year after year, for almost three score years and ten. Twenty million people have read *Little Women* in America alone; and at a recent convention of American librarians, *Little Women* was voted the most popular girl's book in all the world.

When she was a young, exuberant girl, people up in Concord, Massachusetts, thought that Louisa Alcott was "queer." She whistled—and nice girls didn't whistle. She ran races with the boys and held her skirts up above her ankles—and nice girls didn't do that. She even climbed up an apple tree and sat on a limb and read a book. The best people in Concord prophesied that she would come to no good end.

Louisa Alcott was driven to writing in order to help support her sick mother and younger sisters. Her father was an amiable, impractical visionary. He gave a lecture now and then, which nobody really wanted to hear, and got five or ten dollars for it; but, most of the time, he sat at home scratching his elbow and praising the simple life, while his family literally didn't know where its next meal was coming from.

He was a very generous man and he once gave away his last bit of firewood to a needy family. When his wife and daughters complained that their own home was cold, he said: "Now, don't worry. The Lord will send us firewood." So the family went to bed to keep warm.

A driving snow storm swept over New England that night; and when the Alcott family awoke the next morning, they discovered that some farmer had got stuck in the snow with a load of wood, and had abandoned it in front of their house. Louisa's father believed God had sent the wood to him; so he went out and helped himself to it.

When Louisa Alcott first began sending her stories to the publishers, they returned like bouncing balls. Finally, one editor told her that she would never be able to write anything with a popular appeal—and he warned her that she ought to renounce her literary ambitions and stick to her sewing.

The old, white, frame house in which Louisa Alcott lived is still standing in Concord, Massachusetts. Twenty-three thousand people make pilgrimages to that house every year. To many of them, it is all but holy ground, and when I visted that house, I saw a woman literally weeping as she wandered through the rooms where Meg and Jo and Beth and Amy had lived and loved and cried.

An ambitious young man, eager to be a novelist, once asked Louisa Alcott if she would advise him to become an author. "No," she replied. "Not if you can do anything else—even dig ditches."

F. W. WOOLWORTH
400,000,000 nickels = $20,000,000

## WOOLWORTH'S BOSS PAID HIM NO SALARY
## BECAUSE HE WAS SO DUMB

WHEN Barbara Hutton Mdivani became twenty-one years old, she gave a party. She had a Hungarian orchestra in her home, filling the night with soft, exotic music, and famous opera stars singing to her of love and romance. And she had a reason for giving a party. She was inheriting about twenty million dollars.

Where did that twenty million dollars come from? Part of it came out of your pocket.

Barbara Hutton Mdivani is a granddaughter of Frank Woolworth; and every time you spend a nickel in one of Woolworth's five and ten cent stores, a part of your nickel finds its way eventually into the exchequer of this beautiful young woman, with short yellow curls.

How did this girl's grandfather make the millions she is now enjoying? Well, he had one great advantage to start with. He was poor. He lived on a farm up near Watertown, New York, and he was so hard up that he had to go barefooted six months out of the year. He didn't have enough money to buy even an overcoat to keep himself warm during the bitter cold winters.

That poverty did big things for him. It aroused his ambition and filled him with a flaming desire to get ahead. He hated the farm and determined to be a storekeeper; so when he was twenty-one years of age, he hitched the old mare to a sleigh, drove into Carthage, New York, and applied for a job in every store in town. But nobody would hire him. He was too green, too gawky and hay-seedy. He didn't know enough even to get a haircut and to wear a white collar and tie.

Finally, he found a railway station agent who was running a sort of a store on the side. This station agent kept a stock of groceries in a freight shed and Frank Woolworth worked for him for nothing—just in order to get experience.

Later on, he got a job working for a drygoods store. Although he was twenty-one years of age, his employers didn't feel he had enough sense to wait on customers, so they made him come down early of a morning, start a fire, sweep out the store, wash windows and deliver packages. And he wasn't allowed to sell goods at all except during the rush hour at noon. As for salary, his bosses didn't want to pay him anything at all for the first six months. So he told them he had saved fifty dollars during his last ten years on the farm and that that was all the money he had in the world—but he agreed to live on that for the first three months if they would agree to pay him fifty cents a day from then on. When he did get his fifty cents a day, he had to work fifteen hours a day for it—so it figured out to about three cents an hour.

Finally, he got a job in another store at ten dollars a week; and he slept in the basement with a revolver under his pillow to protect the store from thieves. This place proved to be a nightmare. His employer hounded him and scolded him and told him he was no good and cut his salary and threatened to fire him. Frank Woolworth was a whipped man. Realizing he could never make good, he went back to the farm, suffered a nervous breakdown, and for a whole year, he couldn't do a stroke of work.

Think of it! This man who was destined to become the greatest retail merchant on earth, was so discouraged now that he abandoned all thought of trying to get ahead in business, and started raising chickens.

Then, one day, to his great surprise, one of his former employers sent for him and offered him a job. It was a bitter cold day in March, sixty years ago. The ground was covered with three feet of snow. Woolworth's father was taking some potatoes to market that day and so Frank crawled up on the sled and sat on a sack of potatoes and rode into Watertown, New York, to start a career that was to bring him wealth and power far beyond his most fantastic expectations.

What was the secret of his success? Just this: he got an idea—a unique idea. He borrowed three hundred dollars and started a store where nothing cost more than a nickel. That first store was in Utica, New York, and it was a total failure. Some days he didn't take in more than $2.50. Out of the first four stores that Woolworth opened, three of them failed.

Refusing to go into debt, he expanded very slowly at first, opening only twelve stores during the first ten years that he was in business.

Finally, he became one of the wealthiest men in America, built himself what was then the highest office building in the world; paid for it with fourteen million dollars in cash; installed a hundred thousand dollar pipe organ in his home, and began collecting relics of Napoleon.

Years before, when he was a poor young man and had met with defeat so often that he had lost all faith in himself, his mother would come and put her arms around her boy and say: "Don't be discouraged, my son; someday you'll be a rich man. . . ."

## A GANG OF COUNTERFEITERS TRIED
## TO STEAL LINCOLN'S BODY

"Big Jim" Kinealy's gang was one of the cleverest bands of counterfeiters that ever vexed and perplexed the United States Secret Service. Soft-spoken and mild mannered, these crooks had waxed rich and opulent by their illicit traffic in home-made greenbacks. For years their profits had been fantastic. But, by the Spring of 1876, a deadly paralysis was creeping over the gang. Their supply of contraband currency was all but exhausted, and they didn't know where to get more, for Ben Boyd, the master engraver who manufactured their counterfeit bills, had been arrested.

Secret Service men had caught Ben Boyd red-handed, had shoved him into jail at the point of a pistol, and a judge had sentenced him to ten years at hard work behind prison bars, in Joliet, Illinois.

The situation was desperate; so "Big Jim" Kinealy and his gang held a council of war.

Hungry for money and drunk with a sense of their own power, they swore that they would get Ben Boyd out of prison and that nothing could stop them. So, in the Autumn of 1876, they attempted a crime that lashed the nation into a fury and set the blood of ten million men boiling with indignation.

This arrogant gang of counterfeiters planned to steal the body of Abraham Lincoln, stuff it into a long sack,

**ABE LINCOLN'S BODY**
Lay in this coffin which "Big Jim" Kinealy's gang tried to steal

pitch it into the bottom of a spring wagon and gallop, with fresh relays of horses, up to Northern Indiana. There they would hide the body among the lonely sand dunes on the shores of Lake Michigan—bury it with no one to observe them excepting the white sea gulls soaring overhead, and a friendly wind blowing over the lake would soon obliterate all the tell-tale tracks in the shifting sand.

And then, while the nation was in an uproar, these counterfeiters planned to apply the screws and drive a hard and crafty bargain. They would agree to bring back the sacred corpse of Abraham Lincoln only after the Government had turned Ben Boyd out of prison, and handed over a fifth of a million dollars in ransom money. Was the scheme dangerous? Not very, for these shrewd crooks knew that there was no law in the state of Illinois making it a crime to steal a body.

So, on the evening of November 6, 1876, three of "Big Jim" Kinealy's gang, boarded a Chicago & Alton train and headed for Lincoln's home town of Springfield, Illinois.

Before leaving Chicago, they bought a London Newspaper, tore a piece out of it, and stuffed the rest of the paper inside a bust of Abraham Lincoln that stood on the bar of a Chicago saloon that was headquarters for the gang.

The thieves planned to leave the torn piece of the newspaper in the empty tomb as they dashed off with the body, knowing that the detective would eagerly pick up the paper and prize it as a clue. Then, when the country was rocking with frenzied excitement, the counterfeiters would approach the Governor of Illinois, offering to return Lincoln's body.

And how would the Governor know he was dealing

with the proper parties? That would be simple, for the ghouls would produce their London newspaper with a torn page exactly fitting the fragment held by the detectives. The identification would be perfect.

So the sinister plot took form, and the gangsters arrived in Springfield on election night in 1876—a time wisely chosen, for there was raging over the nation that night the most bitterly contested election that had stirred the populace since the bloody days of the Civil War.

The first election returns had already begun to flash over the wires, and Springfield was agog with excitement. Boisterous voters, intoxicated with victory, were parading down the streets and across the square, waving fiery torches, shouting, singing, dancing and piercing the velvet blackness of the night with flames from burning tar barrels and picket fences.

What a fitting time to rifle a tomb! For Lincoln lay buried more than two miles away from all this excitement, deep in the dark and deserted woods.

So, confident of their security, the thieves sawed the padlock off the iron door of Lincoln's tomb, stepped inside, pried the marble lid off the sarcophagus, and lifted the wooden casket half out.

Then, one of the gang, a chap by the name of Swegles, started to get a team of horses which he said was waiting for him in a ravine two hundred yards away.

But this man, Swegles, was not what he appeared to be. He was not a crook. He was, in reality, a stool pigeon—an informer, a detective, employed by the Secret Service. He didn't have any team and wagon waiting; but he did have eight armed detectives waiting for him in another part of the tomb. So, the moment he was alone, he raced around to their hiding place and gave a signal which they had agreed upon—he struck a match, lighted a cigar, and whispered the password—WASH.

The eight Secret Service men, clad in their stocking-feet, rushed out of their hiding-place, each armed with a cocked revolver. Dashing around the monument with Swegles, they plunged into the dark tomb and shouted to the thieves to surrender.

But there was no answer. One of the secret service men lighted a match. There lay the coffin, half out of the sarcophagus. But where were the thieves? Had they escaped after all? The detectives searched the cemetery in all directions. A full moon was coming up over the tree-tops; and the excited detectives got mixed up in the semi-darkness and presently began taking pot shots at one another. The thieves, meantime, who had been waiting a hundred feet away for Swegles to return, dashed off through the oak woods and disappeared into the darkness.

Ten days later, they were caught in Chicago, handcuffed, brought back to Springfield, clapped into jail and surrounded by a battery of guards, day and night.

Lincoln's oldest son, Robert, hired some high priced Chicago lawyers to prosecute the gang. But the learned Chicago attorneys had a tough assignment; for, as has already been said, there was no law in Illinois against stealing a body; and the thieves hadn't actually stolen anything. So they were indicted and tried for conspiring to steal *a coffin* worth only seventy-five dollars.

But delays ensued, and the case came to a tardy trial eight months later. By that time, public indignation had died down; and politics and jealousies and personal enmities were at work to defeat justice.

On the first ballot, four jurors actually voted to turn the thieves loose. After a few more ballots, the twelve men compromised and sent the body-stealing counterfeiters to Joliet prison for only twelve months.

## IF H. G. WELLS HADN'T BROKEN HIS LEG HE MIGHT STILL BE CLERKING IN A DRYGOODS STORE

SIXTY years ago, a group of boys were playing on the streets of a London suburb when an accident occurred. One of the bigger boys picked up a little chap, called Bertie Wells, and tossed him high into the air; but instead of catching Bertie when he came down, the big boy dropped him and broke his leg.

For months, Bertie lay writhing in bed with a heavy weight tied to his leg. But the bone didn't set properly. It had to be rebroken. It was a terrible experience. Little Bertie screamed in agony and terror.

That seemed like a tragedy then, but Bertie knows better now. Today he is one of the most famous authors in the world. You know him not as Bertie, but as Herbert George Wells or H. G. Wells. You have probably read some of his books. He has written over seventy-five volumes; and he himself admits that that broken leg was perhaps the luckiest thing that ever happened to him. Why? Because it kept him confined to the house for a whole year. He devoured every book he could get, because there was nothing else he could do. The result was, he developed a taste for books, a love for literature. He was stimulated. He was inspired. He determined to rise above his humdrum surroundings. That broken leg was the turning point of his life.

H. G. WELLS
He told his mother he would kill himself

## ABOUT WELL KNOWN PEOPLE

Today, H. G. Wells is one of the highest paid authors on earth. He has probably made a million dollars with his pen; yet he was brought up in pinching poverty. His father played professional cricket and ran a little crockery shop that was tottering on the edge of failure. H. G. Wells was born in a small bedroom over that shop. The kitchen was down in the basement. It was a dark, dingy hole, and the only light that filtered into it was through a grating from the sidewalk overhead. One of Wells' earliest memories is of sitting in that dark kitchen and watching people's feet as they shuffled over the iron grating above him. Years later, he wrote about those feet, and told how he had learned to judge people by the shoes they wore.

Finally, the crockery shop failed. The family was desperate, so his mother had to take a job as a housekeeper on a big estate in Sussex. Naturally, she lived with the servants, and H. G. Wells often went there to visit her. And it was there that he got his first peep into English society life—and he got that peep from the servants' quarters.

The future author of *The Outline of History* started out in business life, at the age of thirteen, as a drygoods clerk. He had to get up at five o'clock, sweep out the store, build the fire, and slave for fourteen hours a day. It was drudgery, and he despised it. At the end of one month, the boss fired him because he was untidy and slovenly and troublesome.

Then he got a job clerking in a drug store. And again he was fired at the end of the first month.

He finally got a job clerking in another drygoods store. He had to eat, so this time, he held out a bit longer. But when the floorwalker wasn't looking, he would sneak down into the cellar and read Herbert Spencer.

After two years, he could stand it no longer. So he got up one Sunday morning and, without waiting for breakfast, he tramped fifteen miles on an empty stomach to find his mother. He was frantic. He pleaded with her. He wept. He swore that he would kill himself if he had to remain in the shop any longer.

Then he wrote a long, pathetic letter to his old school master. Wells told him he was miserable, heartbroken, that he no longer wanted to live.

And the school master, to his utter astonishment, wrote back, offering him a job as a teacher.

Presto! That was another turning-point in his life.

Yet H. G. Wells will tell you today, in his thin, high voice, that the long hard years of drudgery he spent in a drygoods store were a blessing in disguise. He is naturally lazy and indolent; and the drygoods store taught him to work.

A few years after he began teaching, disaster overtook him with the suddenness of an explosion. It happened in this way: He was playing football. In the heat and excitement of the game, he was knocked down, trampled on, and almost killed. One of his kidneys was smashed and his right lung was punctured. He was bled white with hemorrhages. The doctors gave up all hope; and for months he lived in fear of imminent death. For twelve terrible years after that, he clung to life as a semi-invalid; and yet, during those years, he developed the ability that was to make his name known throughout the civilized world.

For five years, he wrote furiously. The books and articles and stories that he turned out were dull and amateurish. And he had the good sense to realize it. So he burned up almost everything he wrote.

Finally, in spite of being half an invalid, he got another job teaching. There was a pretty girl in the biology class. Her name was Catherine Robbins. Presently H. G. Wells found that he was far more interested in Catherine than in biology. She was frail and sickly. So was he. They wanted to grab all the happiness they could, at once. So they were married.

That was forty years ago; and, instead of dying, Wells regained his strength, turned out to be a human dynamo of energy and has been grinding out two full-length books each year, books that have sent their reverberations around the world.

Wells' mind is constantly blazing with ideas. He even gets up in the middle of the night to put down stray thoughts in his notebook. And this lazy boy who was once fired because of incompetence as a drygoods clerk, now says that he has enough material in his notebooks to keep him writing books for a hundred and fifty years.

He can write anywhere—in his London workshop, on the train, or under a beach umbrella by the seductive blue waters of the Mediterranean. He rents two villas on the French Riviera. One is a workshop, and the other is a guest house. He writes all day and chats with his guests only in the evening. If he can't go to the station to get them, he does the next best thing—he sends a high-powered car to meet them; and with the car, he sends the key to his well-stocked wine-cellar. His guests are always in good humor when he finally appears.

**MOZART**
He sat with his hands wrapped in woolen socks to keep them warm

## MOZART'S FUNERAL COST $3.10—AND NO ONE FOLLOWED HIS COFFIN TO THE GRAVE

THE late Leopold Auer, the great Russian teacher of the violin, who discovered and trained more musical geniuses than any other teacher of our generation, once told me that if you wanted to be a great musician you had to be born poor. He told me there was something—he admitted he didn't know exactly what it was—but he said there was something buried in the soul by poverty—something mystic, something beautiful, something that developed feeling and force and sympathy and tenderness.

Mozart was so poor he was unable to buy wood to heat the shabby room in which he lived, so he sat with his hands wrapped in woolen socks to keep them warm, while he composed the divine music that was to make his name immortal.

He died of consumption at the age of thirty-five—his vitality lowered by constant cold and hunger and lack of nourishment.

His pitiful funeral cost exactly three dollars and ten cents. Only six people followed the cheap pine coffin—and even they turned back because it started to rain.

Harold Sanford, who was Victor Herbert's most intimate friend, told me that when Victor Herbert first came to America, there were times, between seasons, when he was so poor he had only one shirt, and he had to lie in bed while his wife washed and ironed that shirt.

Remember the song that all of us were singing back in the early days of the World War? "It's a Long, Long Way to Tipperary"? That was probably the most popular war song ever written, and yet the author of it, Jack Judge, in order to make a living, had to run a fish market by day and work as an actor by night.

One of the most popular songs ever composed was "Silver Threads Among the Gold." Hart P. Danks composed that song as a love tribute to his wife, and he sold it to his publisher for only fifteen dollars. Later, he and his wife quarrelled and parted; and he died, only twenty years ago, poor and lonely, in a shabby lodging house in Philadelphia. On a table beside his death-bed was a note bearing these words: "It is hard to grow old alone."

One of the most popular musical selections in the world was written by a butcher's son; and, strangely enough, it was composed out among the corn-cribs and hog-pens of Iowa.

It is called "Humoresque."

There is scarcely a single hour of the day or night but what "Humoresque" is being played somewhere in the world.

It was composed by a Bohemian called Anton Dvorak. He came to this country when he was fifty years old; but he couldn't stand the noise and uproar of New York City, so he went out and lived for a while in Spillville, Iowa—a village so tiny that it doesn't have a railroad nor a paved street, even today.

And yet, while living in Spillville, Dvorak wrote a part of his "New World Symphony," which is one of the most beautiful and exquisite things ever composed by man. Since it was written out in the cornfields of Iowa, Dvorak

## ABOUT WELL KNOWN PEOPLE

thought for a time of calling it the "Spillville Symphony."

Dvorak was born ninety-two years ago in a tiny village in far-off Bohemia. He had very little education and had to work long hours in his father's butcher shop. But as he made sausage, melodies kept running through his mind. As he cut pork chops, songs kept welling up in his heart.

So he left the butcher shop and went to Prague to study music. Money? He didn't have any money except a few pennies which he picked up now and then by playing his violin in the street. He was so hard pressed that he had to live in a garret room in one of the poorest sections of town. Cheap as that room was, he couldn't afford it for himself. He had to share it with five other students.

In the winter, the room was bitterly cold; and his body was sometimes weak from hunger, for he missed meals in order to rent the wreck of an old piano that was so battered that some of the keys wouldn't even play. And, sitting at that piano, in a cold garret room, Dvorak composed many beautiful melodies which were never even written down. Why? Because he didn't have the money to buy even a few sheets of paper. Sometimes he actually picked up waste paper on the street and wrote his music on that.

However, let us not feel too sorry for Dvorak, for his poverty unquestionably helped to bring out his genius.

The next time you listen to Dvorak's "Humoresque," see if you can't detect in it a mystic beauty and tenderness and feeling, put there by a man who had suffered, by a man who had struggled and gone cold and hungry, by a man who had known the depths of despair.

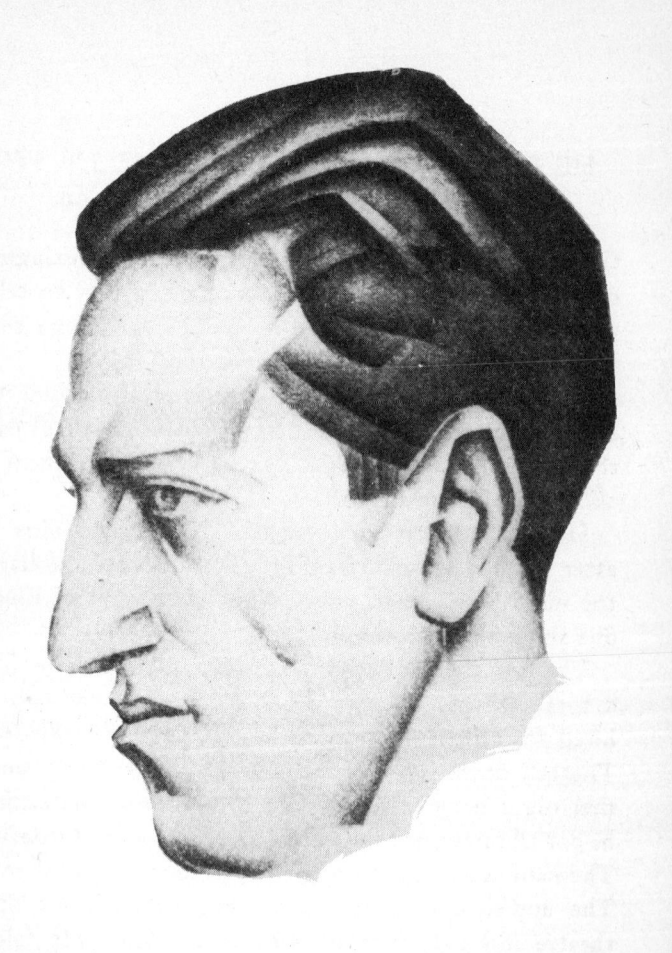

*Courtesy of New Outlook*
**GEORGE GERSHWIN**
He knew what he wanted and went after it—and got it

## HE REVOLUTIONIZED MUSIC BUT HE STILL TAKES THREE LESSONS A WEEK

GEORGE GERSHWIN is perhaps America's most distinguished composer of popular music. I once asked him to tell me the secret of his success; and he said, "That is very simple. I knew what I wanted and I went after it."

And he is still going after it. The most astonishing thing I know about George Gershwin is that he is still taking three music lessons a week—and each one of them lasts about an hour and a half.

He sold his first song for five dollars; and nine years after that, Hollywood paid him fifty thousand dollars for the mere privilege of playing his "Rhapsody in Blue" in one single moving picture.

The first time he ever tried to play in the theatre, he was a total failure; he was almost a disaster. He had been hired for twenty-five dollars a week to play in Fox's City Theatre, down on Fourteenth Street, New York. But the first night he tried to play the music for a vaudeville act, he got all mixed up, and halted and blushed with confusion. The ham actors on the stage joshed him and jeered at him. The audience laughed, and George dashed out of the theatre, his eyes flaming with indignation. He told me recently that that was the most humiliating experience of his life. He didn't even stop to get his pay then, and he has never been back to get it since.

Gershwin wanted to be a painter; and he became a

musician largely because of his mother's jealousy. It happened in this way: Down on the East Side, where the Gershwins lived, the ownership of a piano was the badge of prosperity—the hallmark of financial success. One day, Mrs. Gershwin's sister-in-law bought a piano; and Mrs. Gershwin, George's mother, vowed right then and there that she wasn't going to be outdone by her high-stepping relative who was "putting on the Ritz." So she bought a piano, too. To be sure, it was a second-hand affair, purchased on the installment plan; yet if Mrs. Gershwin hadn't bought that old fashioned upright her son George might never have studied music, the "Rhapsody in Blue" might never have been written, and the history of American music might have been different.

Gershwin wrote and threw away literally hundreds of songs before he scored his first popular hit. "Swanee" was his first success. It was first sung at the Capitol Theatre, on Broadway, New York City, in 1918. But no one paid any attention to it. No one except Al Jolson. Al heard it; and, like the old trooper that he is, he sensed that the song had possibilities.

So, nine months later, when Al Jolson was appearing in a production that needed a song hit, he sang "Swanee," and sent chills of emotion racing up and down hundreds of spines. The audience went wild! In five magical minutes, Al Jolson had turned a song that was a failure into a phenomenal success. In a month, half the nation was singing "Swanee." In two months, millions of people were dancing to it played on phonograph records. George Gershwin was staggered. He had been getting thirty-five dollars a week and now sixty thousand dollars came rolling down upon the author in an avalanche of gold. Sixty thousand dollars? For one song? He didn't know there was that much money in all the world.

George Gershwin is one of the most important figures in the modern theatre; yet he seldom goes to the theatre himself.

Although he has composed melodies that have set millions of couples dancing themselves dizzy, he himself seldom dances.

And he doesn't smoke. He seldom drinks. He works half the night and doesn't get up until noon. He suffers from nervous indigestion, collects French paintings; has a gymnasium in his home, and goes to an osteopath twice a week.

He is a bachelor and he lives in a duplex apartment on East 72 Street, and he never writes "blues" while he is blue.

Lincoln's birthday in 1924 is now regarded by musical critics as one of the turning points in modern American music. Why? Because it was on that day, on a snowy afternoon, that the world first heard George Gershwin's "Rhapsody in Blue." And it really came like a bolt out of the blue.

It was written very largely as a result of an accident. Paul Whiteman asked Gershwin to write a dignified jazz number for his concert; but Gershwin was busy working on a musical comedy. So he forgot all about it. Then one day he picked up a newspaper and was astonished to read that he himself was writing a symphony. Was he? Well, that was news to him. But he said to himself: "All right, I'll do it. I'll show the snooty critics that jazz can be dignified." So he composed the celebrated "Rhapsody in Blue" with astonishing rapidity—composed it in spare hours snatched from other work.

And when the day came for the performance, men and women fought to get in Aeolian Hall, pulling and mauling and tearing at each other as they do at a baseball game or a prizefight.

The concert was a riot. It was greeted with salvos of applause. At last America had broken with tradition and created a new kind of music.

## THEY SPENT THEIR LIVES KEEPING THE
## BIG BAD WOLF AWAY

ARE you in debt? Did you ever lose any money through making a bad investment? Well, if so, you may find consolation in the fact that some of the most brilliant men who ever lived made fools of themselves when it came to investing money. Take Mark Twain for example. He had the ability to make the whole world laugh—or cry; yet when it came to investing money, he didn't have any more sense than you and I had—back in 1929.

He lost almost a hundred thousand dollars in all sorts of inventions, such as steam generators, marine telegraphs, and other marvelous machines that were going to revolutionize the printing industry. There was only one gadget that was too fantastic for Mark Twain to invest in, and that was a queer sort of contraption called a telephone. He was offered a whole hatfull of Bell Telephone stock but he turned it down with a snort—turned down a proposition that would have made him untold millions. Instead, he went into business with one of his relatives—and you know what that means. He lost everything except the kitchen stove.

His friend, H. H. Rogers, of the Standard Oil Company, offered to pay his debts on the basis of fifty cents on the dollar, but Mark Twain wouldn't hear of it. His admirers started a national subscription, and checks came pouring in from all over the country; but Mark Twain

MARK TWAIN
There was only one gadget too fantastic for him to invest in—
and that was the telephone

returned every one of the contributions and insisted on paying his debts himself. He despised lecturing, yet he made a trip around the world, lecturing and living in hotels, suffering from homesickness and boredom. He sacrificed six years of his life to pay his debts, but he finally paid them.

General Grant was brilliant enough to conquer Lee, win the Civil War, and become President of the United States; but he wasn't smart enough to keep out of Wall Street. During the last years of his life, two sharpers got hold of Grant, and persuaded him to go into business with them. Then these men used Grant's good name to manipulate all sorts of crooked deals. These men flim-flammed the public out of sixteen million dollars. When the crash came, Grant, in order to pay his debts, handed over his farm, his houses in Philadelphia and New York, and even the swords and trophies that had been presented to him.

He didn't have a dollar, and he was dying of cancer. He realized that when he was dead, his widow would be poverty-stricken. So, in order to provide for her, he decided to write his memoirs. He dictated until the cancer in his throat got so bad he couldn't speak. Then he finished the book with a pencil—finished it while he was suffering agony. He wrote the last chapter only three days before he died. Mark Twain published the book, and paid Mrs. Grant almost half a million dollars in royalty.

The great Daniel Webster was once sued for nonpayment of a butcher bill.

Oliver Goldsmith, the famous novelist who wrote *The Vicar of Wakefield,* was once arrested because he couldn't pay his room rent.

Balzac, the immortal French novelist, owed so much

money that he was literally afraid to answer the door bell.

Charles the Second, King of England, was so deeply in debt that he gave William Penn all the land that is now the state of Pennsylvania for seventy-five thousand dollars.

Mrs. Abraham Lincoln got so deeply in debt that she had to sell her dresses and furs and jewels. After she left the White House, she was so pressed for cash that she even sold her dead husband's shirts with his initials worked on them.

Whistler, one of America's greatest artists, borrowed money right and left and pawned his pictures to pay his debts. When a creditor came and carried off one of Whistler's chairs, or one of his beds, Whistler would draw a picture of the chair or the bed on the floor—and let it go at that. When the baliff took possession of Whistler's house, Whistler joshed the baliff into dressing up as a butler and serving tea for Whistler and his friends.

Beau Brummel ruled the social life of England a hundred years ago, but he couldn't rule his own bank account. He taught the Prince of Wales how to dress, but he couldn't teach himself how to leave horses and cards alone. When the sheriff broke into the front door, the fastidious Beau Brummel would make a dash for the clothes closet and hide himself behind dresses and petticoats. Finally, he was arrested and thrown into jail for debt.

This man who had once been the perambulating fashion plate of the world, this man whose name even today is a synonym for elegance and perfection in dress, finally became so poverty-stricken that he wore ragged, dirty clothes and was laughed at by the very people whom he had scorned. His mind gave way, and he lived in disgusting filth and finally died in an insane asylum.

Abe Lincoln, as a young man, went into the grocery business with a drunkard as a partner. The store failed, the drunkard died; and left Lincoln all the debts to pay. There was a legal loophole of escape and Lincoln could have avoided paying all of these debts if he had wanted to. But that wasn't Lincoln's way. He scraped and saved and sacrificed for eleven long, hard years until he paid his creditors every dollar that he owed, and he paid them with interest.

Socrates was one of the wisest men who ever lived; yet he was so poor that he had to borrow a chicken now and then in order to have something for supper. When Socrates lay dying, he remembered that he had borrowed a rooster and hadn't paid it back. And the last thing that Socrates ever said on this earth was to ask a friend to pay back the debt of the rooster that he owed.

**BRIGHAM YOUNG**
He attended school for 11½ days, and became one of the outstanding leaders of the nineteenth century

## HE HAD TWENTY-SEVEN WIVES AND MADE TWENTY-SIX OF THEM KNIT THEIR OWN GARTERS

Brigham Young, the great leader of the Mormon religion, married twenty-seven women and made all of them eat at the same table every day, and get down on their knees and pray together every night—and he managed to do this, year after year, without suffering any casualties.

Did I say he got *all* of his wives to eat at the same table? Well, I am wrong. I should have said all, except one. There was a blonde—but I'll tell you about her later.

Why did Brigham Young want so many wives? Was he a lustful, sensuous creature, driven on by physical desires? No. Not at all. He was a very strict and a very religious man. He once said in a sermon: "There are probably few men on earth who care less than I do about the private society of women."

However, the Mormons took the Old Testament literally. They read that Abraham, Isaac and Jacob and Solomon and David had practised polygamy, and they believed that God by a divine and direct revelation had commanded them to marry a number of women and multiply and replenish the earth.

Some of the Mormon leaders openly declared in their sermons that even Jesus had been married to Mary and Martha. They didn't mean that in a sacrilegious way. They believed it with reverence.

Brigham Young once said in a sermon that, if a man didn't believe in the plurality of wives, he would be damned forever and ever; and he also told the bachelors that they would be damned if they didn't get married.

Brigham felt he ought to set a good example to his flock, so he walked out of the house one morning and married a couple of women before lunch. Then he stopped, grabbed a hurried bite, married two more women before dinner, and called it a day.

Brigham Young was forty-four years old the day he married those four women, and one of them was a girl of seventeen. Once, he married a couple of widows. They already had an engagement to live with their first husbands in the next world; so Brigham married them with the distinct understanding that they would be his wives here on this earth only and that they could join their first husbands again in Heaven.

Many Mormon women considered it a great honor to marry Brigham Young. For example, there was Eliza Burgess, a seventeen year old English girl. She fell madly in love with him. She had read in the Old Testament that Jacob worked for seven years without pay to get his wife, so she offered to act as servant in Brigham Young's household for seven years, without compensation, if he would promise to marry her at the end of that time. Brigham, being originally a Vermont Yankee, knew a good bargain when he saw it, so he okayed the proposition and, seven years later, he gave her the keys to Heaven and made her Mrs. Young.

After Brigham had married twenty-four women, he got into trouble. The only wonder is—well, you can finish that sentence yourself. It was 1862, during the Civil War.

Brigham was sixty-one years old, and with two dozen conquests to his credit, you might think he would be willing to settle down and rest on his laurels. But he met a blonde and fell wildly in love with her. Amelia was her name. Amelia, he thought, was different from the others. Of course—she was; they are all different.

Amelia was twenty-five. She had charm. She could play the piano and open her sweet, little mouth and sing a darling song about Fair Bingen on the Rhine. Brigham began to miss meals. He couldn't sleep of nights. He begged her to marry him, but she knew all the feminine tricks; so she stuck her nose in the air and shook her blonde curls. And the more he insisted, the more reluctant she became. Finally, he offered her the keys to Heaven, and said that it was the Lord's will that she should marry him. So she consented.

Then the trouble started. This new blonde who could play the piano and sing about the Rhine, began "high-hatting" the other wives. What? Live under the same roof with the rest of that riff-raff? No sir! Not Amelia. She ordered Brigham to build her a beautiful palace of her own; and he built her a house that was the show-place of Utah for many years.

Would she eat at the same table with those cats that were gossiping about her? No sir! Not Amelia. She condescended to eat in the same room with them, but she had a little, private table of her own at the head of the room, and she made Brigham take his meals with her; and, according to gossip, she sometimes feasted on prairie chicken while the others worried along on salt pork.

Brigham had been brought up in pinching poverty. As a boy, he had even made his own straw hats, so he **was** always lecturing to his wives about economy. He gave them wool and told them to knit their own garters; and he threatened to divorce them if they didn't stop buying velvet ribbon and quit spending so much money on the whims of fashion.

Did Amelia knit her own garters? She hooted at the idea. She played the piano and bought silks and satins and perfumes and jewelry and swanked around town in her own private carriage and made the other wives sit behind her when they went to the theatre.

If there had been any shot guns allowed in the Brigham Young household, I opine that a certain blonde would have awakened one morning and found herself dead.

Brigham once announced in a sermon that if any of his flock were troubled and would consult him, he would be glad to give them the word of the Lord on the question. One day, a troubled, old lady asked Brigham whether the Lord wanted her to wear red or yellow flannel next to her skin. Brigham thought a minute and then said: "Yellow, by all means."

Another old lady rushed to him in tears because her husband had told her to go to hell. Brigham patted her arm and said solemnly, "Now, don't go. Don't go."

Brigham Young had fifty-six children. His favorite wife bore him ten children, and eleven of his wives gave him no children at all. Sometimes his household saw the birth of three babies in one month. Once, two of his wives presented him with children on the same day. His last child was born when he was sixty-eight.

He established a private school for his own children, and offered a black, silk dress to the first daughter who could take down one of his sermons in shorthand.

I have been gossiping, rather flippantly, perhaps, about Brigham Young's family life. But there is a far more significant side to his career. He attended school for only eleven and a half days in his entire life; yet he became one of the outstanding leaders of the nineteenth century. William H. Seward who was Lincoln's Secretary of State, declared that America never produced a greater statesman than Brigham Young.

The story of how this self-taught, Vermont Yankee led a bewildered and persecuted people across the parched plains in ox-carts and covered wagons and settled them in a barren and unexplored region, and irrigated the desert, and made it blossom like the rose—the story of how he built there a great economic empire, and made himself the high priest of a new religion, and nourished it, and caused it to spread like a green bay tree—the story of how he did all this is one of the few great dramas of our past.

CORNELIUS VANDERBILT
His son's horses were faster than his

## HE SLEPT WITH EACH LEG OF HIS BED IN SALT TO KEEP EVIL SPIRITS AWAY

How would you like to have someone hand you forty million dollars? Well, that is precisely what happened to young Alfred Gwynne Vanderbilt on his twenty-first birthday.

Strange as it seems, this young man, who was heir to one of the largest fortunes in America, has never gone to college. And apparently he never intends to go, for he is educating himself with private tutors as he roams around the world. He recently took a fishing cruise in the Caribbean Sea, and he has also penetrated into the wildest part of Africa and has taken motion pictures of lions and giraffes and elephants in their native haunts.

He doesn't give two whoops for Society; but, like all the Vanderbilts, he is intensely interested in horse racing, and he inherited one of the most valuable racing stables in America.

His father, Alfred Gwynne Vanderbilt, Sr., went down on the *Lusitania* when it was torpedoed by a German submarine during the war. Although he was a noted sportsman, he was unable to swim. As the *Lusitania* was sinking, he was given a place in one of the life boats; but after he had taken his seat, he got out and gave his place to a woman. Shortly afterwards, another hysterical woman ran around the deck, tearing her hair and screaming that she had no life-belt. So Vanderbilt took off his life-belt and gave it to her.

A few minutes later the ship went down; and Vanderbilt died like the true sportsman and gentleman that he was.

The Vanderbilt fortune was founded by old Cornelius Vanderbilt. What a funny codger he was! There still is a bronze statue of him on the front of the Grand Central Station, on Forty-second Street, New York.

Born on a farm in Staten Island, about a hundred and forty years ago, he borrowed one hundred dollars from his mother, on his sixteenth birthday, bought a small ferry boat and started carrying passengers from Staten Island to New York.

How much do you suppose he made out of that hundred dollar start? One hundred millions! That is all. How did he do it? Largely by investing in ships and railways.

In spite of his vast wealth, he always lived economically. For example, during his last illness, his physician said he ought to have some champagne. "What!" he cried, "Champagne? Great Scott, Doctor, I can't afford champagne. Won't sody water do?"

He wasn't joking. He was serious.

When he was first married and struggling to get a start, his wife ran a hotel in New Brunswick, New Jersey; and, in her spare time, she raised a family of eleven children. She dreamed then of the time when they might have money and she could take it easy; but after her husband became the richest man in the world, she often said that the happiest days in her life had been those spent back in New Jersey, when she was poor and running a hotel and struggling to raise a family.

When old Cornelius got rich, he wanted to move to the city, but his wife was an old-fashioned, home-loving person; and she objected. They quarreled, and he told her she was crazy; and, in order to prove it, he had her shut up in an insane asylum for a year.

He thought that his oldest son, Billy, was worthless; thought he would be no good whatever in business; so he kept Billy on the farm until after he was forty years of age.

Then Billy began to show his cleverness. For example, the old man sold Billy fertilizer at four dollars a load. Cornelius thought, of course, that his son meant wagon loads. But Billy fooled him. Billy took a whole barge load off the old man's ship and paid him only four dollars for it. Old Cornelius was beaten, but he admired that sort of shrewdness; and he also admired fast horses. When Billy's horses began to run faster than his, the old man was positive that his son was brilliant. So he took Billy off the farm, and finally put him at the head of the New York Central Railroad. When the old man died, he left Billy ninety million dollars. And when Billy died, he left a fortune of two hundred million.

The old man had a lot of eccentricities. He never used a check book. He always wrote his checks on half-sheets of ordinary writing paper. And he hadn't the slightest respect for the opinions of others. Even when he was eighty-four years old and prostrate on his death bed, old Cornelius Vanderbilt refused to be bossed. When the nurses and doctors tried to make him do things, he threw hot water bottles at them. For weeks before he passed away, newspaper reporters swarmed about the house waiting for news of his death. That made him angry; and one day, when one of the reporters rang the door bell, he crawled out of bed, dragged himself to the head of the stairs and shouted: "I hain't dead and I hain't goin' to die."

When he was ill, he hired spiritualists and mediums to talk to his mother who had been dead forty years; and when his dead mother "told him" to put mustard plasters on his aching back, he paid more attention to her messages than he did to his doctors.

He always revered the memory of his mother; and, years after she passed away, he would have rockets shot off in her honor whenever his palatial steam yacht passed his mother's old farm on Staten Island.

With his vast wealth, he was one of the most powerful men in America. He was afraid of no one. Yet he had each leg of his bed set in a dish filled with salt, to keep the evil spirits from attacking him while he slept.

## SHE WROTE MYSTERY STORIES—SO THE GHOSTS DECIDED TO MOVE RIGHT IN

Millions of people have read the stories of Mary Roberts Rinehart. She has written forty-four books and thousands of pages of magazine fiction; yet she started writing when she was the mother of three babies—not because she cared about fame, but because she was driven frantic by debts.

The first story she ever sold brought thirty-four dollars; but editors are glad to pay thirty-four thousand dollars now for one of her serials. She is one of the most highly paid authors in America and also one of the most prolific; yet she says that "writing is sheer, grinding drudgery."

She once sold big bundles of her stories to the movies for seventy-five dollars a bundle; but later on, she refused an offer of fifty thousand dollars a year to go to Hollywood and write stories for the screen.

Mrs. Rinehart was tortured by an apparently unending siege of operations. But she kept right on writing—in beds and wheel chairs and in hospitals. She once wrote poems while she was convalescing from diphtheria; and she had to fumigate the manuscript before she could mail it out to an editor.

Mary Roberts Rinehart has often remarked that, if she hadn't had so much illness to keep her in bed, she would never have written so many books.

The poems that she fumigated didn't sell. In fact, almost none of her poems sold. She once wrote a book of poems

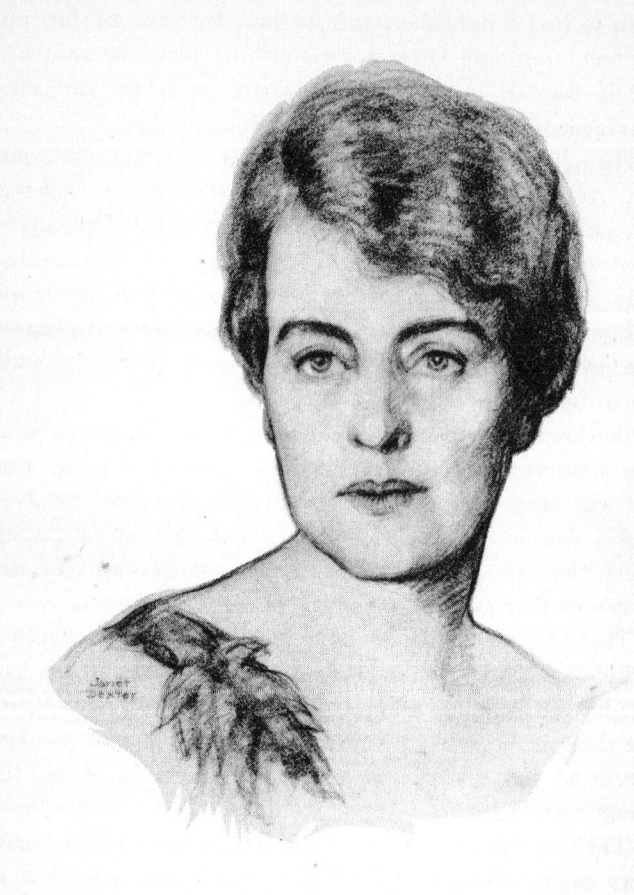

*Courtesy of Farrar and Rinehart*
**MARY ROBERTS RINEHART**
She fumigated her poems before she mailed them

for children and made a trip from Pittsburgh to New York to find a publisher, and she literally wore blisters on her feet, tramping from one publishing house to another, but it was all in vain. Going home, whipped and discouraged, she abandoned all thought of writing.

Then, suddenly, with the swiftness of a tornado, she was overwhelmed by a financial catastrophe. It was the old, old story. Wall Street! Too many stocks! Thin margins! A panic! Everything lost in a day! All her savings gone and the family smothered under twelve thousand dollars of debt. She was appalled. Twelve thousand dollars! She declared it might as well have been twelve million! The situation seemed utterly hopeless.

She longed to do something to help her husband, who was a physician. But what? She thought of writing. But she was busy with housework all day, and dead tired at night. And even after she went to bed, she had to get up every two hours to heat milk over a gas jet and feed her under-nourished baby.

Then, one evening, Doctor Rinehart came home from a sick call and told her a strange story: a patient of his had lost his memory and imagined himself a young man again. He thought his wife was a strange woman and he laughed when he was told that the children running about the house were his own.

The case fascinated Mrs. Rinehart; so she sat down that very night, wrote it into a short story, and mailed it to Munsey's Magazine; and, to her surprise, the magazine not only accepted the story and sent her a check for thirty-four dollars, but also a letter asking for more stories.

So she started writing in her spare time. And if you think she had much spare time, listen to this schedule.

She kept a three-story house immaculately clean, from top to bottom, and took care of her husband and three growing sons. To be sure, she had a servant to help her; but she did all the family shopping herself and planned and helped to prepare three meals a day. She even put up home-made jellies and pickles and jams for the family; did all the mending, and sewed most of her own clothes and most of her children's clothes; and, for fourteen years, she cared for her mother, who was a helpless invalid. She made out the bills for Doctor Rinehart, did his book-keeping, and often she assisted him in emergency cases. The only time she ever had for her writing was in the evening when her husband was out visiting his patients.

Yet, one year from the time that Mary Roberts Rinehart started out to write, she had sold forty-five stories and made more than eighteen hundred dollars—a remarkable feat.

She has lived in two "haunted" houses. One on Long Island, and the other in Washington.

Shortly after Boise Penrose died, the Rinehart family moved into his apartment in Washington, and Mrs. Rinehart occupied the room in which he died. Immediately strange things began to happen.

The bell in the bedroom rang repeatedly when no one was near. Doors swung slowly open when no one was behind them. Birds and bats mysteriously appeared in her room when the door and windows were locked and there was no chimney through which they could enter. Sinister rappings played a ghostly tattoo on the head of the bed; and, in the dead of night, the doors were pounded vigorously.

The keys of the typewriter rattled and banged at two

## ABOUT WELL KNOWN PEOPLE

o'clock in the morning when no earthly hands were near them. The dog would start into an apparently empty room; and then wheel and come crawling out on his stomach, his hair bristling and his eyes filled with terror.

Once, a huge potted plant was found sitting upright in the middle of the living room floor, sitting there without its crock, thirty feet away from the place where it belonged. Chairs and tables moved about and the night was filled with weird and ghostly sounds.

Mrs. Rinehart was alarmed. She began to sleep fitfully. A friend who was a spiritualist advised her to speak to the spirits when she heard these noises—yes, she was to speak to the spirits and ask what they wanted and what she could do to help them.

The next night, a living room window closed itself, apparently without any earthly aid; so Mrs. Rinehart crept out of bed, edged into the living room with her back against the wall and then spoke in a frightened, trembling voice to the spirits from another world.

Instantly, a bell started ringing down the hall—ringing and clattering like a fire alarm.

She was frightened almost into hysterics until she suddenly realized that she herself was leaning against the bell button on the wall.

Mrs. Rinehart doesn't believe in ghosts. She doesn't believe that the spirit of Boise Penrose was haunting the house. But to use her own words: "There were times, I admit, when I wondered if some small imp from an invisible world was playing and frolicking among us."

*Courtesy of The New Yorker*
THOMAS A. EDISON
Doctors looked at the shape of his head and predicted brain trouble

## THOMAS EDISON WASN'T THE ONLY SMART MAN WITH A BAD MEMORY

One day when I was having lunch at the Vanderbilt Hotel, in New York, I noticed that when the coat room girl took my hat, she didn't give me a check for it. I was a bit surprised and I asked her why; she said it wasn't necessary to give me a check—that she would remember me—and she did. She told me that she had often taken the hats and coats of two hundred strangers, stacked them up in a pile and handed each man the right coat and the right hat as he walked out. I talked to the manager of the hotel and he told me this girl hadn't made a memory mistake in fifteen years.

I doubt whether Thomas Edison could have accomplished a feat like that even if you had offered him a million dollars. Edison had a very poor memory—especially in his youth. In school, he forgot everything he was taught, and he was always at the foot of his class. He drove his teachers to despair. They declared that he was addle-brained, that he was too stupid to learn, and the doctors even predicted he would have brain trouble, for his head had an extraordinary shape. As a matter of fact, he attended school only three months during his entire life. After that, his mother taught him at home; and what a magnificent job she did, for he all but transformed the world in which we live.

Yet, later in life, Thomas Edison developed a remarkable memory for scientific data, and he mastered most of the scientific facts in his vast private library. He developed an extraordinary ability to concentrate, to forget everything but the subject he had in hand.

One day, while he was deeply absorbed in trying to solve some scientific problem, he went to the court house to pay his taxes. He had to stand in line for some time; and when his turn came, he actually forgot his own name. One of his neighbors, seeing his embarrassment, reminded him that his name was Thomas Edison. He afterwards declared that he couldn't have called his name for a few seconds then even if his life had depended upon it.

At one time he seriously thought of studying some system to improve his memory.

Edison frequently worked in his laboratory all night long. One morning, while he was waiting for his breakfast to be brought to him, he fell asleep. One of his assistants, who had just eaten some ham and eggs and was feeling in a jovial mood, wanted to fool the old man; so he placed his empty tray of dishes on the table in front of Edison. A few minutes later Edison awoke, rubbed his eyes, and looked down at the bread crusts and the empty plate and the empty coffee cup. He thought a moment and then came to the conclusion that he must have eaten breakfast before he had his nap; so he pushed back from the table, lighted a cigar, had a smoke, and started to work again and never knew the difference until his assistants broke into an uproar of laughter.

Asa Gray, the famous American botanist, was able to call from memory the names of more than twenty-five thousand plants; and according to his biographers, Julius Caesar was able to call from memory the names of thousands of his soldiers.

## ABOUT WELL KNOWN PEOPLE

Babe Ruth, on the other hand, finds it difficult to remember either names or faces. He goes about speaking to almost everyone, knowing that he may possibly have met them at some time or another.

Charlie Chaplin had a private secretary and press agent for seven years. He traveled with him constantly; and yet this secretary, Carlyle Robinson, told me that, at the end of those seven years, Charlie Chaplin didn't know his last name.

The second largest university in the world is a Mohammedan college in Cairo, Egypt. The entrance examination to this University requires every student to repeat the Koran from memory. The Koran, which is the Mohammedan Bible, is almost as long as the New Testament, and three days are required to recite it. Yet, every one of more than twenty thousand students regularly accomplish that feat.

Lord Byron boasted that he could repeat all the verses that he ever wrote; but Sir Walter Scott, on the other hand, had a very poor memory. He once praised one of his own poems very highly, thinking that Byron had written it.

Lord Bacon was able to dictate one of his most famous books from memory; but Joseph Jefferson, on the other hand, played "Rip Van Winkle" almost every night for a dozen years and kept forgetting his lines right up to the very end.

When Abraham Lincoln wanted to memorize anything, he read it aloud so that he would impress it both on his sense of sight and his sense of hearing.

Macaulay, the great English historian, had perhaps the most remarkable memory of any man who ever lived. He could look at a page of print and photograph it on his mind almost as accurately as a camera could do it. He could read a chapter of a book only once and repeat it from memory. He wrote histories without even having to refer to reference books, and his biographers declare that in order to win a bet, he learned "Paradise Lost" in one night.

Calvin Coolidge used to read a few pages of "Paradise Lost" every night before going to sleep. Well, if you are troubled with insomnia, try "Paradise Lost." It is better than sleeping powders.

Thousands of people have had remarkable memories. Theodore Roosevelt was one of them. He was intensely interested in meeting people. He found out little personal details about the people he met, studied their faces, their mannerisms, and repeated their names until they were indelibly impressed upon his memory. This helped him enormously in his political life. He made people feel immensely important by calling their names the second time he met them.

He once surprised a Japanese banker, whom he had not seen for fifteen years, by beginning to talk immediately about a subject that they had discussed fifteen years previously. When Roosevelt read anything he wanted to remember, he got a deep, vivid impression. By persistence and practice, he trained himself to concentrate under the most adverse conditions. In 1912, during the Bull Moose Convention, in Chicago, his headquarters were in the Congress Hotel. Crowds surged through the streets below, crying, waving banners, shouting "We want Teddy!" "We want Teddy!" The roar of the throng, the music of bands,

## ABOUT WELL KNOWN PEOPLE

the coming and going of politicians, the hurried conferences, the consultations would have driven the ordinary individual to distraction; but Roosevelt sat in a rocking chair in his room, oblivious to it all, reading Herodotus, the Greek historian.

On his trip through the Brazilian wilderness, as soon as he reached the camping ground in the evening, he found a dry spot under some huge trees, got out a camp stool and his copy of Gibbon's "Decline and Fall of the Roman Empire" and, at once, he became so immersed in the book that he was oblivious to the rain, to the noise and activity of the camp, to the sounds of the tropical forest. It is small wonder that a man with such powers of concentration was able to remember what he read.

George Bidder was a wealthy Englishman who died fifty years ago. When he was only ten years of age, he figured out in his head in exactly 121 seconds how much the interest would be on 4444 pounds for 4444 days at 4½ per cent per annum.

A man died out in Coldwater, Michigan, not long ago—a picturesque character called "Railroad Jack." He had an astonishing memory; and, for twenty years, he traveled from one college town to another, amazing the students. He would go into a restaurant where the college boys were eating and say, "I'm 'Railroad Jack.' Ask me anything about any character in history, and I'll give you the facts." Naturally, the boys tried to show him up. They would ask him some absurd question such as "How old was Socrates' wife when she married?" And he would answer, quick as a flash: "Socrates didn't marry until he was forty; and then, in spite of his wisdom, he married a flapper who was only nineteen." Or they would ask him where bayonets were first used, and he would tell them immediately that "it was at the battle of Killiecranke in Scotland, on the 27th day of July, 1689." Naturally the boys would buy him a lunch and then take up a collection and buy him a suit of clothes.

Henry Ford was so impressed with his ability that he gave him a car so that he could travel about giving his sidewalk lessons in history. But he refused to use the car, and continued to travel around in a cart. One the side of the cart he had painted the words "RAILROAD JACK— HISTORICAL GENIUS."

"Railroad Jack" died in an old, abandoned building at seventy nine years of age. He willed his body to the University of Michigan so the medical school could examine his brain and try to discover the secret of his memory. I wrote to Professor W. B. Pillsbury, head of the Department of Psychology at the University of Michigan, and asked him to tell me the secret of "Railroad Jack's" amazing memory. Professor Pillsbury told me that "Railroad Jack" had devoted years of his life to learning one definite group of facts until he had accumulated a staggering quantity of them. He also told me in his letter that a lot of these mental marvels with amazing memories have been investigated, and that some of them were endowed with extraordinary intelligence but that an equally large number of them were almost feeble-minded.

That means that if you have a brilliant memory, you may be approaching genius or you may be only two jumps ahead of the lunatic asylum. Figure it out for yourself.

Well, if your memory is as bad as mine, cheer up, for

Leonardo da Vinci was one of the most distinguished men who ever lived, and he couldn't remember anything unless he made a note of it—and when he *did* make notes, he lost them, even as you and I.

*Courtesy of A. L. Burt Co.*
O. HENRY
Five years in jail gave him the leisure to write

## THEY WENT TO JAIL—AND IT ADDED
## TO THEIR GREATNESS

WHO do you suppose was the most famous short story writer who ever lived? You have read his stories. More than six million copies of his books have been sold; and they have been translated into almost every language on earth, including the Japanese, Esperanto, Czecho-Slovakian, Danish, Norwegian, French, German, Swedish and Russian. His pen name was O. Henry, and he was born about seventy years ago.

O. Henry's life is a striking illustration of a man who battled against tremendous odds and succeeded, in spite of terrible handicaps.

First, he had the handicap of very little education. He didn't even attend high school; and he never saw the inside of a college; yet today his stories are studied as models of good writing in half the universities of the land.

Second, he was handicapped by the ravages of diseases. The doctors feared that he was going to die of consumption; so they took him away from his home in North Carolina, sent him down to Texas, and he got a job herding sheep on a ranch there.

Today, automobile tourists drive hundreds of miles out of their way to see that ranch; and as they approach it, they halt their cars and walk reverently over the ground where O. Henry once tended his flocks.

Third, he had the apparent misfortune of being thrown into prison. It happened in this way:

After he regained his health, O. Henry got a job as a cashier in a bank in Austin, Texas. The cowboys and sheep men in that section had the habit of walking into the bank when the clerks were busy and helping themselves to as much cash as they wanted, signing a receipt for it, and then going on about their business.

Suddenly, one day, a state bank examiner came to town, inspected the bank's cash—and found money missing. O. Henry, the cashier, was arrested. He was hauled into court; and although he probably had never taken a dishonest dollar himself, nevertheless he was sent to prison for five years.

That prison sentence seemed like a calamity at the time; but, in a way, it was most fortunate; for O. Henry began writing, in prison, the brilliant stories that were destined to make his name honored and loved wherever the English language is spoken. It is quite probable that he would never have written at all if he hadn't been sent to prison.

I was talking to Warden Lawes, of Sing Sing, recently; and he told me that almost every man in Sing Sing wants to write the story of his life. In fact, so many of the prisoners in Sing Sing want to write, that the prison school gives them a free course in short story writing. Naturally, very few of them succeed, but nevertheless, it is a fact that many well-known men have written in jail.

For example, Sir Walter Raleigh, the famous dandy, who wore diamonds in his shoes and pearls in his ears; Sir Walter, the gallant *courtier* who tossed his cloak into a mud puddle for Queen Elizabeth to step on—even he wrote in jail. He was kept behind prison bars for fourteen terrible years because of political jealousy.

His cell was damp and narrow, and the walls oozed

## ABOUT WELL KNOWN PEOPLE

muddy water. He suffered terribly from the cold. His left arm became stiff with rheumatism. His hand was gnarled and drawn with pain. But in spite of his misery and heartbreak, he wrote a history of the world while in prison—a history that is being studied in our schools and colleges even today—three hundred years after it was written.

For twelve years, John Bunyan was locked up in a jail —locked up because of his religious teachings. While in prison, he made lace to buy bread for his wife and four hungry children. But while his hands were busy making lace, his mind was busy with great thoughts; and there, in his cold, dark, damp dungeon, he wrote a book that almost every student in America has read. It is called *Pilgrim's Progress*, and it had been translated into more languages than any other book that ever existed, with the exception of the Bible.

Cervantes wrote *Don Quixote*, one of the great books of all time, in jail. Voltaire wrote in jail. Oscar Wilde wrote in jail. Eugene V. Debs wrote in jail. More than a million copies of Adolf Hitler's biography have been sold; and Hitler wrote part of that book in jail. In fact, I have just about come to the conclusion that if you want to write a book, it might be a good idea to smash a window and get yourself locked up.

When Richard Lovelace was thrown into an English prison, two hundred and fifty years ago, he glorified his dungeon by writing one of the well known poems of the English language. It is a love poem that he wrote to his sweetheart. It is entitled: *To Althea from Prison*.

> Stone walls do not a prison make,
> Nor iron bars a cage,

The spotless mind, and innocent,
Calls that a hermitage,
If I have freedom in my love,
And in my soul am free,
Angels alone that are above,
Enjoy such liberty.